Foreword

One of the most challenging child protection issues of our time has been the realisation that children can be most vulnerable to abuse in the places where they ought to be safest. One public inquiry after another has catalogued the physical, sexual and emotional abuse too often experienced by children in residential care, boarding schools and other services where they have been sent for their own safety, treatment or education. When an allegation or suspicion of possible abuse arises in a residential or day care service, local authority child protection procedures may require an independent element to investigate the allegations, particularly where its own staff fall under suspicion. As a result of increased awareness of the need for vigilance, many voluntary agencies now provide specialist services for independent enquiries under Section 47 of the 1989 Children Act. This report describes the NSPCC experience of carrying out independent Section 47 enquiries, and the lessons learned as a result.

Because independent enquiries are a new feature of child protection services, few guidelines are available, and the research identifies some of the difficulties which this can cause. Most previous social work experience has been of enquiries into possible abuse within families. The guidance and practice standards so developed are in some ways inappropriate for the very different conditions in an institutional setting, where the situation is likely to be far more complex, may involve many more adults or children, and where the relationship between abuser and victim will be fundamentally different. The report highlights the lack of research on institutional abuse in Britain and the resulting problems in developing evidence based practice in protecting children or dealing with abuse when it occurs.

The research findings indicate the need for greater clarity over the objectives and conduct of independent enquiries at the point of commissioning, to ensure that the remit is adequate and flexible. This is a two way process in which the local authority commissioner and the independent agency both need to play their part. There may be pressures of many kinds on investigators which have to be managed carefully if they are not to undermine the independence and integrity of the enquiry. Additionally, the plan for the investigation must provide for good communication between agencies throughout, and support to both children and staff involved. Most importantly, there must be a clear plan of action to deal with the findings of the enquiry, whatever they may be. The research produces worrying indications that social workers carrying out independent enquiries often felt that no action had been taken on their recommendations, leaving children to face continued risk of poor care and possible abuse. The paramount consideration in any enquiry into child abuse must be to ensure the present and future safety of the children involved.

Although this report charts the experience of the NSPCC, discussions with other agencies suggest that the findings given here are part of the experience of many providing independent enquiry services. We have found the report very useful in planning the future development of the NSPCC services. We hope that it will be of similar value to other agencies and contribute to standard setting in these difficult investigations.

Jim Harding
Director and Chief Executive

Acknowledgements

The author would like to thank Dr Pat Cawson and Dr David Berridge for their help, support and constructive comments throughout the research project. Thanks also to Caroline Boyle for her invaluable secretarial support and to Sheila Murphy for her much appreciated time spent on proof reading this report. The author is especially grateful to all the NSPCC practitioners and managers who agreed to give up their time to participate in the research.

[illegible] search Series

Investigating Institutional Abuse of Children

An Exploration of the NSPCC Experience

by Christine Barter

The author

Christine Barter is an NSPCC Research Fellow affiliated to the University of Luton. She has previously worked on a range of projects concerning the experiences of adolescents, including young people who run away, and protecting children and young people from racism and racial abuse. She is currently working on a study focusing on physical and sexual violence amongst young people within residential children's homes.

NSPCC

The National Society for the Prevention of Cruelty to Children (NSPCC) is the UK's leading charity specialising in child protection and the prevention of cruelty to children.

The NSPCC exists to prevent children from suffering abuse and is working for a future for children free from cruelty.

First published 1998 by the NSPCC
42 Curtain Road
London
EC2A 3NH

Tel: 0171 825 2500
Fax: 0171 825 2525
Email: nspcc-research@mailbox.ulcc.ac.uk

Registered charity number 216401

Director and Chief Executive: Jim Harding

ISBN 0 902498843

Design by Red Stone

Contents

Tables

Summary of research and findings

The following section provides a brief overview of the main findings of the research as they relate to each chapter.

Institutional abuse: the context

This chapter presents the main themes relating to the institutional abuse of children and documents the relevant guidance and legislation.

Methodology

The research criteria for inclusion in the study was any NSPCC teams who had undertaken an independent investigation into abuse within a residential or day care setting between 1994 and 1996. Overall 16 projects were identified, and a total of 41 semi structured interviews undertaken with NSPCC employees. The majority (26) were with practitioners, 12 were with team leaders and 3 with managers above project leader level. In addition, 36 independent investigation reports undertaken in the two year period were analysed.

Background information: findings from the investigation reports

- Thirty-six independent investigations concerned 76 allegations of abuse made by 67 children and young people against 50 alleged abusers (40 adults and 10 residents).

- The highest number of children involved in any one investigation was 15, however the great majority (25) involved only a single child.

- Two-thirds of investigations related to recent abuse, 8 concerned past abuse, and 4 involved both.

- The majority of children involved were adolescents, with an equal number of boys and girls.

- Nearly all of the allegations concerned abuse within residential children's homes.

- Nearly all the alleged perpetrators were male.

- The majority of allegations related to physical abuse (33), followed by sexual abuse (24), inappropriate restraint (16) and a minority concerned inappropriate care.

- Just over half (41) of allegations were upheld, a third (26) were deemed inconclusive and 9 allegations were found to be false.

Evaluation of the investigation process

Strategy meeting

Nearly every person interviewed (38) stated that at the beginning of the investigation a strategy meeting had been convened which they, or another representative of the NSPCC had attended. The importance of such meetings, especially the preliminary one, to the smooth running of the investigation, was emphasised by nearly all these respondents (36). Although in principle this meeting is supposed to aid multi-agency working, in practice many respondents (28) had found it to be a highly politicised process where the agenda had often been pre-determined by the local authority representatives. Some (19) reported feeling intimidated by their lack of status within these meetings due to the seniority of the local authority representatives present.

Remit and scope of the investigation

The remit and scope of the investigation was a central concern of many respondents, mostly this focused on how encompassing the scope of the investigation should be. A minority (9) felt that it should be strictly limited to the child protection instance that had been alleged. However the majority of respondents (26) who expressed a view felt that the remit should not simply focus on the specific incident, but needed to have a significantly more extensive scope enabling the wider dynamics of the establishment, including the role of management, to be evaluated.

In practice many (24) identified that the remit they had worked with in the past had been too restrictive, with the majority of respondents reporting that they would have preferred to have a broader remit, which included a mandate to interview all staff, including management, and any children whom they felt would be appropriate.

Suspension

About half (21) of the alleged adult abusers had been suspended during the investigations. In the majority of these cases (15) staff members had been suspended prior to the initial strategy meeting. Workers were most likely to be suspended in cases of alleged sexual abuse. However NSPCC investigators frequently stated that suspension was sometimes viewed by both the suspended staff member and other members of the residential staff team as a verdict of guilt without a trial. Some investigators (15) felt that this actually made the staff view them with suspicion and affected their willingness to co-operate with the investigation.

Multi-agency working

In only two investigations the social service department, the police service and the NSPCC each provided a number of workers to undertake a multi-agency inquiry. Both of these investigations concerned widespread sexual abuse allegations, covering a number of years. Although a further 19 investigations did have some level of police presence, their participation was minor and quickly fell away at the initial stages when no criminal prosecution was thought likely to occur. In 8 investigations, NSPCC practitioners worked alongside colleagues from social services departments, generally child protection officers. In 12 investigations two or more NSPCC practitioners worked on the inquiry, and in 14 cases a single NSPCC practitioner undertook the investigation.

The nature of independence

Evaluation of the NSPCC's independent status

The majority of respondents (34) voiced some doubts about how independent they were from the commissioning local authority. All respondents felt they were able to bring higher levels of independence than if the local authority concerned used its own child protection workers to undertake the investigation. However, respondents frequently (19) felt that projects' service-level agreements with commissioning local authorities sat uncomfortably alongside notions of independence. Just over half (22) felt that local authorities placed pressure on them to accept an investigation, and many (26) reported feeling that refusing a request would have repercussions regarding their wider working relationships with the authority concerned. Respondents (21) also reported feeling worried they might jeopardise their projects' relationship with the local authority if they *'rocked the boat too much'* within the investigation. Some respondents (9) stated that their projects had developed positive relationships with the local authorities, where each respective body had clear expectations about each other's role, and the level of autonomy NSPCC investigators required. However most reported this had taken a considerable amount of time to develop.

Investigating colleagues

The research found that the most commonly stated problem (28) concerned investigating professionals within the team's own geographical area. This was additionally compounded in many cases by investigating professionals who were working in a field related to their own. Respondents were particularly uncomfortable with investigating professionals whom they knew through their general work.

Previous knowledge about a facility

About a third of respondents (13) felt that having previous contact with a residential establishment, even if this did not include direct contact with the alleged abuser(s), might affect their ability to view the situation objectively. Primarily, respondents expressed concern about bringing prior knowledge, and preconceptions about a facility into the investigation, and the effect this may have on their ability to be impartial and objective.

Effect on wider working practices

About two-thirds of respondents (24) were worried that undertaking these investigations might affect their wider relationship with colleagues. It was feared that workers who had been investigated might discuss this with colleagues outside their facilities, which could affect the team's relationships with other professionals. Some respondents (8) discussed difficulties in resuming a working relationship with colleagues they had investigated, irrespective of the verdict.

Investigating peers outside local areas

Teams that investigated agencies outside their immediate areas stated that this had made their role as investigators significantly easier, more impartial and less stressful for themselves and the workers they were investigating.

Evidence

Most investigations lacked physical corroborative evidence. In only 14 cases did the abuse result in a recorded physical injury. There was therefore a reliance upon witness statements and the accounts of the child and the alleged abuser. In recognition of this, respondents felt that the interviewing techniques used in independent investigations were not only extremely important but also significantly different to family investigations. The major differences revolved around the *'detective style'* interviewing required when investigating out-of-home abuse compared to the more *'assisting'* interviews undertaken in cases of suspected intra-familial abuse.

Issues of support

Many (32) felt that the young people who had alleged the abuse incident(s) were not properly supported throughout the investigatory process. In a minority of investigations (6) the child had been formally supported by a social worker or the local authority's children's rights officer, however these cases generally seemed to be the exception. Most (34) respondents felt that these would be the most appropriate link person to provide this service to the complainant.

Supporting the alleged abuser

Although most respondents placed priority upon providing support for the young person concerned, many (27) also felt that the alleged abusers were often simply abandoned, with no support being offered from the local authority. The research showed that only rarely (8) did the local authority appoint a formal link person for the alleged abuser. Even in instances where such support was received, it was limited, and often seemed to simply disappear as the investigation proceeded.

Supporting other children

The research also showed that many respondents (18) felt that the young people within the homes were not being properly supported through the process. Allegations of abuse may be particularly difficult for vulnerable children to deal with, especially if it raises issues relating to their past abuse.

Supporting the staff group

Respondents (23) felt that facilities were often forgotten, being offered very little, if any, support from their immediate line managers. In addition advice or guidance was rarely offered informing staff of their responsibility to support the alleged victim and other children within the home.

Post-substantiation issues

Most respondents (31) felt that a central feature of an investigation was to determine and highlight which policies, procedures and working practices may have contributed to the abuse occurring. Leading on from this, some respondents (26) felt that the report should not simply identify the present policy and practice issues, but ought to contain specific recommendations as to how these could be changed to ensure that the abuse would not occur again for similar reasons.

However, many respondents (33) stated that the post-substantiation phase of the investigation was *'unsatisfactory'*, *'highly frustrating'* or *'inadequate'*. Most felt that in comparison to investigating intra-familial abuse there existed a lack of post-substantiation procedures.

Development issues

Respondents had generally not received any specialised training regarding investigating out-of-home abuse. The majority of workers felt that the skills they had acquired in relation to family abuse were relevant to investigating institutional abuse allegations. Nevertheless, many respondents stated that they would welcome additional training. Training requirements centred upon the differences between intra-familial abuse and institutional abuse, residential policies and procedures, informal institutional processes, restraint techniques and interviewing adolescents with emotional and/or behavioural difficulties.

1 Institutional abuse: the context

Introduction

Over the last 10 years a number of *'scandals'* concerning the abuse of children in residential settings have received both professional and public attention and concern. Various inquiry reports have been undertaken, generally in response to the occurrence of widespread abuse within residential settings. These inquiries, reviewing retrospectively the events and factors that allowed children in different institutions to be abused, often over many years, have consistently reported upon the inadequate responses made by local authorities in reply to children's and young people's allegations of abuse (Levy and Kahan, 1991; Kirkwood, 1993). Criticism has been especially levelled at the investigations that were undertaken in response to such allegations: specifically, that when children told of the abuse they were experiencing within their placements, their accusations were rarely taken seriously. It appears from the inquiry reports that investigations were frequently viewed by the local authorities concerned as little more than a paper exercise, often with senior management showing very little commitment either to the process or the outcome. One may possibly deduce from this, that if the independence of such investigations had been properly secured, with thorough investigations being undertaken, the abuse of these children might have been uncovered sooner. Thus not only might their abusive experiences have been substantially lessened, but additionally, other children that followed might have been spared the abuse they in turn suffered.

Despite the substantial number of such *'scandals'* over the last ten years, and their subsequent inquiries, very little UK research has been undertaken regarding the institutional abuse of children, including the role of independent investigations. Subsequently very few protocols have been developed within the UK to guide practitioners involved in undertaking such investigations into out-of-home abuse. An exception is the *Castle Hill Report* (Brannan, Jones, and Murch,1993), which arose from the experience of investigators undertaking the Castle Hill Inquiry who were unable to find any formal guidance to assist them in identifying the extent of the problem, or in formulating an investigation plan. The team documented their experiences and from this produced a practice guide for professionals involved in future large scale investigations surrounding the widespread abuse of children.

This lack of research means that we are generally ignorant of the factors associated with abuse within residential or day care settings within the UK, including the prevalence of such abuse, or how effective different procedures and mechanisms are in protecting children from the different forms of abuse found within residential settings. We also have very few first hand accounts of this form of abuse to shape our perceptions and understandings or to inform possible responses. For an example of young people sharing their experiences see: Safe and Sound, *So Who are We Meant to Trust Now?* (1996). Similarly, very little is known about the abusers themselves, although some case studies have recently been undertaken (Colton and Vanstone 1996).

As Doran and Brannan (1996) argue, this lack of systematic research is in itself a complicating factor when attempting to respond to abuse within institutions, creating an obstacle to formulating effective investigative procedures. The authors state that:

"Because there is no central mechanism in this country for reporting or recording investigations and findings regarding institutional abuse, we remain ignorant of its true scope. Until there is compulsory recording and reporting of all investigations and findings, and such data is centrally compiled, it will not be possible to gauge the extent of institutional abuse...Continuing ignorance of the scale of abuse, combined with an inability to negotiate the difficulty and complexity of this area, means that it is impossible to plan for it organisationally, emotionally and professionally. This means we continue to be both reactive and uncoordinated. This is exacerbated by the skill and cunning employed by child abusers to perpetrate their crimes." (p157)

They continue that:

"The effective prevention and investigation of abuse within institutions is dependent on an ability to understand and address the complex and multi-faceted nature of their internal and external hierarchical and power systems. An awareness of the relationship between these aspects is critical to the establishment of appropriate and objective preventative or investigative techniques." (p159)

Due to the absence of such research and practice literature in this country we must largely rely upon research based on the American experience, where many states have developed specialised teams to respond to and investigate this form of abuse. Although responses vary between states, and some have still to develop a specialised service, their general experiences can still inform our own. However, we need to be cautious when transferring findings based on the American experience. Firstly, the nature and types of institutions will be significantly different to our own, in both their function and size. American institutions are often significantly larger than those found within the UK. Secondly, the wider social and cultural dynamics within which institutions are embedded will be significantly different in the US. These factors need to be taken into account when viewing the North American research evidence. In addition, the definitions of institutional abuse adopted within the US literature also warrant some consideration prior to observing the research findings.

Definitions

Within the US research and practice literature the issue of definitions has been an important element in discussions relating to the institutional abuse of children. Similarly, the recent Department of Health's *Child Protection: Messages from Research* (1995a) has also emphasised the importance of definitions, although specifically in relation to familial abuse. This recognises that discussions surrounding definitions are not simply an abstract theoretical debate, but are central to both policy and practice developments:

"Any discussion of child abuse and child protection services will benefit from agreements about definition. Unfortunately, there is no absolute definition of abuse." (p11)

Messages from Research stresses that what is abusive needs to be viewed in the context of what is *'ordinary'* behaviour in families. The usefulness of this child abuse perspective when transferred on to abuse in out-of-home settings is however debatable. Such an approach would entail conceptualising abuse within institutions in the context of what is *'common'* behaviour within such facilities. However, *'ordinary'* behaviour within residential settings may not necessarily always be in the best interests of children. As *Messages from Research* reminds us in relation to family behaviour, what is deemed normal because it is exhibited by the majority of parents is not necessarily *'optimal'*.

Messages from Research additionally states that:

"...child abuse is not an absolute concept. Most behaviour has to be seen in context before it can be thought of as maltreatment. With the exception of some sexual abuse, it should always be clear that maltreatment is seldom an event, a single incident that requires action to protect the child." (p14)

Again, although this may be true of abuse within families, when transferred to abuse within an institutional environment it becomes problematic. Staff working with children need to be held to a higher standard of care than parents (Rindfleisch, 1990). Parents have a heightened level of discretion in their child rearing practices compared to residential workers, including the level of basic care and supervision, degree of privacy, etc. Consequently, an isolated incident by a member of staff may require a child protection response.

As Thomas (1982) postulates, residential abuse differs from familial abuse in that the severity of the abuse is irrelevant, as is evidence in support of wilful intent. The State Institutional Abuse and Neglect Advisory Committee (1987) similarly state that mitigating circumstances, intent and severity are not relevant criteria for determining child abuse and/or neglect in residential settings. Facilities must ensure in advance that the child care environment is harm free - it is therefore irrelevant if the abuse occurred accidentally or that mitigating circumstances were present. It is important to remember when viewing institutional abuse incidents that the effect on children of being abused within an environment that is supposedly there to protect them, irrespective of the severity, may be devastating to the young person. Therefore, although the degree of severity is obviously important, acts which may seem less significant to an external observer may not be viewed in this way by the child or young person concerned, especially if they are in public care following previous abuse in their families.

These factors illustrate some of the differences in defining and responding to abuse within families and abuse within residential settings, and emphasises the need to concentrate initially upon the issue of definitions.

Gil (1982) provides a commonly acknowledged starting point, supplying a broad definition of institutional abuse:

"...any system, programme, policy, procedure or individual interaction with a child in placement that abuses, neglects, or is detrimental to the child's health, safety, or emotional and physical well-being, or in any way exploits or violates the child's basic rights." (p9)

Gil identifies three discrete forms of institutional abuse. The first is '*overt*' or '*direct abuse*', consisting of any sexual, physical or emotional abuse of a child by a worker, very similar to familial abuse. However, the second two forms that Gil identifies are unique to institutional settings. '*Programme abuse*' consists of an institution's regime or treatment programme which, although accepted by staff, to an external observer would be viewed as abusive (the so called *'Pindown'* scandal is an example of this). The third form of abuse Gil defines as '*system abuse*':

"...perpetrated not by any single person or programme, but by the immense and complicated child care system, stretched beyond its limits and incapable of guaranteeing safety to all children in care." (p117)

Gil provides a wide definition of institutional abuse, resting on a child welfare rather than a child protection perspective. Some definitions have been narrower and do not include child welfare elements, whilst others reject the concept of system definitions (for example Thomas, 1990). From this country NAYPIC (National Association of Young People in Care, 1989) have also argued for a broad definition of institutional abuse, based on a child welfare position, to be adopted. They state that institutional abuse occurs when:

"...a system becoming increasingly more punitive in its failure to respond to their (children's) need." (p1)

Others have however argued that vague definitions of institutional abuse can play a role in facilitating maltreatment and in hindering its reporting and investigation (Besharov, 1987; Rindfleisch and Rabb, 1984a). It is therefore apparent that the choice of definition can have an immense impact on our understanding of the extent and nature of out-of-home maltreatment. Nevertheless despite these divisions, there does appear to be a generally agreed core element to all definitions, centring upon the difference between institutional and familial abuse.

As Westcott (1991) reflects:

"Generally, there has been consensus among authors in defining the abuse that takes place, and such definitions have served to emphasise the differences between familial and institutional abuse that must be considered." (p9)

The uniqueness of certain forms of institutional abuse have implications for the expertise and training that practitioners involved in investigating this form of abuse require, and for the formulation of practice guidelines and the development of appropriate protocols. These will be considered throughout this report.

Lastly, the difference between children and young people making a complaint about their quality of care under the Children Act 1989, as opposed to an allegation of abuse, needs to be briefly considered. Many issues relating to the quality of care a child or young person receives, for example, being placed inappropriately due to a lack of resources, would be defined as constituting institutional abuse within the child welfare perspective. However, under the Children Act 1989, such issues are dealt with by the local authorities' complaints procedures and not through the process of independent investigation. *The Children Act 1989 Guidance and Regulations, Volume 4: Residential Care* (Department of Health, 1991a) states:

"A complaint is a written or oral expression of dissatisfaction or disquiet in relation to an individual child about the local authority's exercise of its function under Part III and paragraph 4 of schedule 7 of the Children Act 1989 and matters in relation to children accommodated by voluntary organisations and registered children's homes. A complaint may arise as a result of an unwelcome or disputed decision, concern about the quality or appropriateness of services, delay in decision-making about services or about their delivery or non-delivery." (para 5.5c)

Consequently, many types of situations which, if viewed from a child welfare standpoint would constitute system abuse, will fall outside the criteria for an independent investigation, and therefore will not be included in this research. This must be borne in mind when considering the findings of this study, and especially when viewing the material relating to the investigation reports contained in Chapter 3.

US research

American research into the incidence rates of institutional abuse has consistently highlighted two main themes; firstly that children in residential facilities are more vulnerable to abuse than those who live in families, and secondly, that the under-reporting of abuse incidents within residential settings is a common occurrence. Lerman (1994), on reviewing the available data, concludes that children in out-of-home placements have a greater or equal chance of being victimised by maltreatment than children living in their family homes. In contrast, some authors have stated that institutional abuse rarely occurs. Matsushima (1990) felt that outright abuse was uncommon within residential settings, and that physical maltreatment particularly was a rare phenomenon. Unfortunately, this position is not reflected in the majority of research findings.

When viewing the incidents and prevalence rates of institutional abuse, we need to have a clear understanding of what thresholds are being employed, compared to those relating to familial abuse, and the effect this will have upon the level of abuse uncovered. Some professionals have argued that family members have more latitude in the treatment of their children than do institutional personnel and thus, behaviour which may be classified as mistreatment by institutional staff may not be so classified when employed by parents or family members. As the Department of Health's *Child Protection: Messages from Research* (1995a) states:

"...the amount of abuse in society depends upon the point at which thresholds are drawn. Move the dividing line upwards and the amount of abuse in society diminishes; a downward movement has the opposite effect... the amount of abuse covered by child protection agencies may increase or decrease depending on the drawing of the threshold." (p15)

With the above in mind, the New York State Commission on Quality of Care (1992) described abuse rates within their mental health facilities as being as high as 87 reports per 1000 children. This figure contrasts sharply with the 28 non-institutionalised children reporting per 1000 in New York State (New York State Commission on Quality of Care 1992). In their landmark study, Rindfleisch and Rabb (1984b) undertook the first comprehensive study to assess the level of abuse in residential facilities across ten US states. They found 25 to 55 reports (average 39) of maltreatment per 1000 children, with confirmed complaint rates of 5 to 30 (average 10) per 1000. Similarly Groze (1990) using data from a single state showed a reporting rate of 587 per 1000 and a confirmation rate of 85 per 1000. As Nunno (1997) reports, these discrepancies in perceived and actual incidence rates provide gist for the conflict to continue among professionals concerned with the welfare of children in out-of-home care. Rindfleisch and Rabb (1984b) also found that fewer than one in five complainable situations in out-of-home placements were being reported to the appropriate authorities.

The lack of comparable evidence relating to the incidence of abuse within UK institutions means it is impossible to speculate on the level of training and specialised services that are required. Furthermore, without understanding the nature of such abuse, we cannot begin to strategically formulate and develop the appropriate services for the children and young people concerned.

Official guidance

The official literature governing the reporting and investigation of abuse within institutions in England and Wales is mainly contained in two sources of Department of Health guidance which relate to the Children Act 1989: *The Children Act 1989 Guidance and Regulations, Volume 4: Residential Care* (Department of Health, 1991a) paragraphs 1.179 to 1.192, and *Working Together Under the Children Act 1989: A guide to arrangements for inter-agency co-operation for the protection of children from abuse* (Department of Health, 1991b) sections 5.20 to 5.22. The section on organised abuse contained within the latter guidance is also very pertinent to abuse by staff in residential care.

Working Together Under the Children Act 1989 states:

"Investigations of allegations or of suspicions of abuse by members of the Social Service Department's (SSD) own staff should, as far as possible, include an independent element. This could, for example, be a representative from another SSD or the local NSPCC. Wherever possible, the investigation of the allegations or suspicions should also be carried out by a senior member of the social services department who does not have immediate line management responsibilities for the home in which the alleged incident has occurred." (5.20.6)

Similarly, *The Children Act 1989 Guidance and Regulations, Volume 5: Independent Schools* (Department of Health, 1991c) also highlights the importance of child protection in such settings:

"To ensure, as far as possible, that the welfare of pupils is secured, schools should have clearly laid down and recognised procedures for dealing with allegations of abuse. These could reflect the procedures laid down in the Area Child Protection Committee (ACPC) for the locality in which the school is situated. The investigation of possible abuse is a matter for the SSD once they have been informed, (unless the local ACPC procedures state otherwise: it can for example sometimes be the NSPCC or, in some kinds of cases the police)." (para 3.2.2)

The Department of Health's (1991d) *The Children Act 1989 Guidance and Regulations, Volume 6: Children with Disabilities*, although providing detailed and valuable guidance relating to complaints procedures, and child protection in relation to court orders, does not include specific direction on child protection concerns arising within residential settings for children with disabilities. Presumably the guidance in Volume Four covering residential care is judged to be adequate, however this may be a false assumption. As Marchant and Page (1992) emphasise, although in many respects disabled children are just like other children, they may have particular needs in relation to the investigation of abuse, as well as being particularly vulnerable to abuse. For example, severely disabled children may be unable to communicate to others that they are being mistreated, or be unaware what certain behaviours entail. Some disabled children require personal intimate care, which brings a heightened opportunity for sexual exploitation. Marchant and Page (1992) emphasise the importance of adapting the investigation procedures to the particular needs of the child, in particular the assessment of suspicion and preparation for interviewing. Although the principles of good practice in relation to investigating abuse apply equally to all children, those with disabilities require specific child protection strategies (Kelly, 1992; Westcott and Cross, 1996).

Within our study none of the children involved in any of the investigations were identified as having physical, sensory and/or intellectual impairments. Consequently, this research is unfortunately unable to make any significant contribution to investigating institutional abuse allegations concerning children and young people with disabilities. Possible explanations for the absence of disabled children within the NSPCC investigation sample are discussed in Chapter 4, in connection with the local authority response to allegations of institutional abuse.

Official guidance also stipulates that any investigation into institutional abuse must comprise a three strand investigation. This is highlighted in both *The Children Act 1989 Guidance and Regulations, Volume 4: Residential Care* (Department of Health, 1991a) and *Working Together under the Children Act 1989: A guide to arrangements for inter-agency co-operation for the protection of children from abuse* (Department of Health, 1991b). The latter states:

"(a) First, there is the child protection investigation, which will be undertaken in accordance with the procedures then in place for dealing with such matters, including a child protection conference, and decisions taken on the action necessary to ensure the continued protection of the child concerned.

(b) Secondly, the circumstances may require a police investigation of whether a crime has been committed.

(c) Thirdly, the employer's disciplinary procedures should be invoked to ascertain whether there has been misconduct or gross misconduct on the part of the staff member." (para 5.20.11)

The Children Act 1989 Guidance and Regulations, Volume 4: Residential Care (Department of Health, 1991a) stresses that all three strands of the investigations must be viewed independently of each other, crucially the levels of proof needed in each of the strands are substantially different and must be applied separately to each:

"It is essential that the common facts of the alleged abuse are applied independently to each of the three strands of investigation. The fact that a prosecution is not possible, does not mean that action in relation to child protection or employee discipline is not feasible or necessary. The outcome of one strand of investigation may have a bearing on another. The important thing is that a definite conclusion is reached in each case." (para 1.189)

This research focuses exclusively upon the child protection strand of the investigation process, although in a minority of cases a criminal investigation did run alongside the child protection investigation.

2 Methodology

Research aims and objectives

The aim of the research was to document the NSPCC experiences of undertaking independent investigations into allegations of abuse within residential and day care settings. The main objectives of the study focused on observing the process involved in undertaking such investigations; exploring the experiences and perceptions of both practitioners and managers involved in this role; evaluating the difficulties they faced; ways in which they felt the process may be improved; and to identify any possible service provision issues raised for the NSPCC.

Research methodology

The research criteria for inclusion in the study were that any NSPCC teams should have undertaken an independent investigation into abuse within a residential or day care setting within the previous two years, between 1994 and 1996. Although to some extent this cut off point was arbitrary, the pilot stage of the research found that practitioners were generally unable to recall investigations before this deadline in sufficient detail. Investigations into abuse in foster care were not included as the dynamics in these settings are more similar to familial contexts than residential ones.

Thirty-three projects which met the above criteria were directly contacted after being located through the NSPCC's Child Information Data System (CIDS) database, which provides information on all case work, including investigations, undertaken by all NSPCC teams. Unfortunately, the CIDS database does not have a search format to identify independent investigations into allegations of institutional abuse. This meant that some projects could have been missed out when searching this database. In view of this, all teams who stated in their project's aims that they provided an investigation service were also contacted, even if they had not been identified through the CIDS database. In addition the teams themselves identified other projects which they believed might have been involved in this form of work. Lastly, there appeared a feature in *Link*, the NSPCC's child protection research group's information newsletter, which is distributed to all NSPCC projects, asking teams who fitted the research criteria to contact the research group. Overall 16 projects (from over 120) were identified which fitted the criteria, and all agreed to participate in the study. These teams provided a wide variety of different children's services, ranging from comprehensive assessments, therapeutic work, to children's rights services and consultancy. Overall, 6 of the projects stated that the provision of independent investigations was one of their team's main objectives.

Information was collected through unstructured and semi-structured interviews, mostly undertaken in person although a few were conducted over the telephone. Interviews predominantly involved only one person being interviewed at a time. However in 3 cases at the request of the workers involved, or due to exceptional circumstances, 2 or more members of staff were interviewed jointly. All respondents were reassured of the confidential nature of the research, emphasising that they would not be identified within the report, or by any other means. The total number of interviews was 41. The majority (26) were with practitioners, 12 were with team leaders and 3 with managers above team leader level.

In addition, 36 investigation reports undertaken by the above teams over the two year period were analysed. Fifteen were undertaken in 1994, 17 in 1995 and 4 up to May 1996. The highest number of investigations undertaken by any team in the two year period was 5, with the most frequent number being 2. These 36 investigations concerned allegations made by 67 children against 50 alleged abusers. The highest number of children involved in any one investigation was 15, however the great majority (25) involved only a single child.

Methodological considerations mean that caution should be shown in interpreting the findings from the investigation reports. Due to the unrepresentative nature of the sample, no attempt should be made to generalise these findings regarding prevalence rates or the nature of such abuse. However, when these findings are viewed in relation to the central research aims of this study, they do provide an important insight into the type of allegations that commissioning local authorities decide require an additional element of independence.

Young people's views

The aim of the research was to document the NSPCC experiences of investigating institutional abuse allegations. Consequently it was outside the remit of this project to include the views and evaluations of the young people involved in these investigations. This is a significant omission and needs to borne in mind when viewing the research findings. As the young people were located in numerous local authorities throughout England and Wales it would not have been possible to gain access to them, indeed many may have moved placements, local authorities or have left social care altogether. Ethical considerations were also present, as these young people had been through a very difficult time they might not wish to be contacted concerning this. However, the importance of young people's own assessments, perceptions and recommendations cannot be under-estimated.

3 Background information: findings from the investigation reports

This chapter focuses on the 36 investigation reports undertaken by the 16 teams over the two year period covered by the research. In total this involved 67 children, making a total of 76 allegations, against 40 members of staff and 10 other residents, within 37 settings (one investigation concerned two establishments). As the research is focusing upon the process of the investigation itself rather than the actual abuse incidents, all reports were analysed irrespective of their outcomes.

The settings investigated

The vast majority of settings investigated (35) were residential children's homes. Most of these (32) were described as local authority *'ordinary'* homes for adolescents. In addition, one secure unit was investigated; a residential home for both younger children and adolescents: and one home run by a voluntary organisation. In two separate cases allegations related to very young children placed in local authority day care nursery provision.

The cases

The length of investigations, from initial strategy meeting to completion of the investigation, ranged from between 3 days to 10 months, with the modal length of time being between 3 to 4 weeks. Twenty-four of the investigations concerned allegations about present abuse, 8 related to past abuse, and 4 to both past and present abuse.

The majority (59) of allegations were reported by the young people themselves. However, in a number of instances someone other than the young person made the allegation of abuse. In 3 cases this was the young person's parent; in 2 the referrers were direct care residential workers; and there were also individual examples of a child's social worker, a children's rights worker and a domestic member of staff.

Investigation outcomes

Just over half (41) of the children's allegations were upheld by the investigation team. However, in a third (26) the outcome of the investigation was inconclusive, with 9 deemed to be untrue. It is important to remember that an inconclusive finding does not mean that the young person's claim was found to be false, but that the investigators were unable to accumulate enough substantial evidence to either prove or disprove the allegation. Unfortunately, the limited sample size prohibits any more detailed analysis being undertaken surrounding the degree of substantiation in relation to the nature, type and source of allegation.

Of the 9 false outcomes; 3 young people stated that they had lied about the allegation (only one stated a motive which was to provide support for another resident's allegation of abuse which was subsequently found to be true); 2 separate investigations concerning inappropriate touch found that the young person's past experiences of sexual abuse had severely affected their ability to judge what was inappropriate contact; 3 investigations concerning inappropriate use of restraint concluded that the type and level of restraint was consistent with guidelines and was a suitable response to the situation; one allegation of neglect was found to be untrue (although another allegation by the same child was found to be true).

Cavara and Ogren (1983), discussing child protection investigations into allegations of abuse by foster carers, found that initially there existed a large number of *'unable to substantiate'* findings. Workers relied too heavily upon facts that could be proven, but hesitated to rely upon their professional judgements in drawing conclusions from these facts.

Studies within the US have also raised concern about the level of substantiation in institutional abuse investigations. Nunno and Rindfleisch (1991) for example drew attention to the low average substantiation rate of 27% for out-of-home investigations. Other studies have also reported rates of substantiation, from 14% (Groze 1990), 23% (New York State Commission on Quality of Care, 1992), to as high as 42% (Spencer and Knudsen, 1992). In comparison the *'confirmation'* level of 54% found within this research appears to be relatively high. However due to the very small sample size, and the difference between the UK and the US, we are unable to draw any conclusions from this.

The children

Of the 67 children involved in the investigations, 34 were boys and 33 were girls. Table 1 provides a further breakdown of age by gender.

Table 1 Age of children when alleged abuse occurred by gender

Age (years)	Boys	Girls	Total
2	1	1	2
10	0	1	1
11	1	1	2
12	1	2	3
13	5	3	8
14	8	6	14
15	11	14	25
16	4	2	6
17	3	3	6
Total	**34**	**33**	**67**

Age of children

Over half of the children involved in investigations were aged between 14 and 15 years. Over two-thirds of children were between the ages of 13 and 16, with the mean age being 14. Previous research into institutional maltreatment has overwhelmingly found that the vast majority of children and young people experiencing this form of abuse are adolescents. Groze (1990), for example, found that 75% of their sample were over 14 years old, with the mean age being 14.6 years. However, as Blatt (1992) speculates, the age distribution within these institutional maltreatment samples is reflective of the general ages of the resident population surveyed. The Department of Health (1995b) statistics show that 63% of children living in community homes were between the ages of 10 and 15, with 88% being between 10 and 17 years old.

Table 2 Type of abuse allegations

Abuse type	No of allegations	
Physical abuse	33	(43%)
Sexual abuse	24	(32%)
Inappropriate restraint	16	(21%)
Neglect / inappropriate care	3	(4%)
Total	**76**	**(100%)**

More than one form of abuse was alleged per child

Type of institutional abuse allegation

The above table shows that the most frequently investigated allegations concerned physical abuse, followed by sexual abuse. Together these constitute two thirds of all allegation types. The use of inappropriate restraint was alleged by nearly a quarter of children. However, only a minority of investigations related to allegations of neglect or inappropriate care. Within the US research no clear pattern has emerged regarding the type of abuse children in residential facilities most commonly report. For example Blatt (1992) states that the majority of allegations in the study concerned lacerations (35%, presumably related to physical abuse), followed by inappropriate restraint (22%) and then sexual abuse (17%). Rosenthal et al (1991) also found physical abuse to be the most commonly alleged (55%), followed by sexual abuse (24%) and thirdly neglect (21%). In contrast Blatt and Brown (1986) report that neglect was most often reported (64%), then physical abuse (24%) and lastly sexual abuse (10%). Groze (1990) in comparison found that over half of all allegations (55%) related to inappropriate treatment. Despite the inconsistencies in these findings, if we compared them to those contained within this study it is evident that allegations concerning inappropriate care and/or neglect are generally absent from the investigations commissioned.

Range of allegations

The abuse allegations ranged widely in their level of severity. Physical abuse allegations included being pushed, thrown against walls and doors, children having their heads hit against floors or walls, being kicked by workers and being slapped. Sexual abuse allegations mostly concerned inappropriate touching, being hugged in a sexual way, being kissed on the body/lips, workers deliberately entering/staying in a child's room while they were undressed or dressing, being talked to in a sexually explicit manner. Children also alleged having pornographic photographs taken, having their sex organs touched/fondled, being forced to touch a worker's sex organs, forced to perform oral sex, and attempted or full sexual penetration.

Inappropriate restraint allegations generally concerned restraint that had caused pain to a child, or methods of restraint that were not acceptable to the child, or lasted too long, or used too great a level of force. Children also complained about being restrained when they felt it was not appropriate to their behaviour at the time of the alleged incident. The minority of neglect and inappropriate care allegations included workers being *'drunk and disorderly'* whilst on duty, withholding medication and not responding to the medical needs of a child, and a worker speaking to a child in a consistently critical and disrespectful way over a number of months.

Table 3 Type of abuse allegation by gender of child

Abuse type	Male	Female
Physical abuse only	20	6
Sexual abuse only	4	13
Restraint only	8	4
Physical and sexual abuse	0	5
Physical abuse and restraint	1	1
Sexual abuse and restraint	0	2
Neglect / inappropriate care	1	2
Total	**34**	**33**

Gender differences in allegations of abuse

Differential patterns of abuse allegations were found to exist for male and female children. Most of the allegations made by boys which were investigated concerned physical abuse, while allegations by girls more often concerned sexual abuse. Overall, 21 boys compared to 12 girls made allegations involving physical abuse, with 20 girls alleging sexual abuse compared to only 4 boys. Interestingly, more girls alleged multiple forms of abuse compared to boys, although numbers are too small to enable any firm conclusions to be drawn.

The relationship between gender and abuse type had been identified within previous research on out-of-home abuse. In the USA Groze (1990) for example found that males were over-represented in physical abuse and inappropriate treatment allegations, with girls being predominantly involved in allegations of sexual abuse. Rosenthal et al (1991) identified that boys reported higher levels of physical abuse (71%), and neglect (76%), whilst girls most frequently reported sexual abuse (60%).

Table 4 Position of alleged abuser by gender

Position of alleged abuser	Male	Female	Total
Residential direct care worker	21	9	30
Residents	9	1	10
Officer in charge	5	0	5
Assistant officer in charge	2	0	2
Domestic staff	0	2	2
External persons	1	0	1
Total	**38**	**12**	**50**

Gender of alleged abusers

The above table clearly shows that more males than females are implicated in abuse allegations. Overall, two-thirds of allegations against an adult concerned a male member of staff. If this is viewed alongside the fact that the majority of direct care residential work is undertaken by a female workforce (Balloch et al, 1995; Sinclair and Gibbs, 1998; Berridge and Brodie, 1998) it is clear that males are proportionally over represented.

Blatt (1992) also found an over-representation of male workers in his US maltreatment sample, with over three-quarters of children identifying their perpetrators as being male. In comparison only a third to a half of residential workers were male. Rindfleisch and Baros-Van Hull (1982) found that female residential workers were less likely to use force in their work compared to male members of staff.

Status of alleged abusers

Table 4 also clearly shows that the majority of allegations were against workers of direct care level. Previous studies have documented the association between the status of workers within facilities and levels of abuse. Direct care staff have more contact with children than those with managerial roles, consequently they have more occasions to abuse them. Workers most at risk of using greater levels of force are those who have little or no input into the decision making process (Rindfleisch and Baros-Van Hull, 1982 and Sundrum,1984). These are generally direct care workers who are often external to the decision making process. It has been suggested that workers with little power over their own lives will seek to reduce their feelings of powerlessness by targeting those who have even less control, which will inevitably be residents (Mercer, 1982).

Both US research studies and UK evidence has highlighted the link between institutional maltreatment and the lack of appropriate training, especially surrounding crisis management (Blatt, 1990; Dodge-Reyome, 1990; Levy and Kahan, 1991; Department of Health, 1991e). Residential direct care workers are often inadequately trained and lack appropriate social work qualifications. For example, a survey conducted for Utting's (Department of Health, 1991e) review of residential care found that 70% of staff lacked any form of relevant qualifications. However we need to be cautious in presenting solutions to institutional abuse solely in terms of heightened training and qualifications. Both Sinclair and Gibbs (1998) and Berridge and Brodie (1998) found that professional qualifications *per se* were not *directly* related to quality of care measurements. However professional training is still important. The latter authors conclude that although clarity in orientation and working methods were the main factors accounting for quality of care variations within their sample of children's homes, stability in staffing was also revealed as an important variable. The existence of a positive training policy may be a central aspect in achieving this stability.

Sir William Utting (Department of Health, 1991e) stated:

"The reality is also that advances brought about by improvements in pay, conditions of service and training will prove temporary unless they are co-ordinated within a strategy to improve the standing of residential child care as an occupation. Staff need to be assured that what they are doing is valued, important and will endure."(p17)

However past inquiry reports (Levy and Kahan, 1991; Kirkwood, 1993) have highlighted that management is not necessarily always a protective factor. Similarly, in this research 14 % of allegations were against workers of assistant or officer in charge level. None of the investigations related to managers above this position.

Table 5 places the type of abuse allegations and sex of the child in context of the worker's sex. The data pertaining to each category is very small, consequently it is not possible to generalise from these findings. Nevertheless they do illuminate the kind of allegations that were investigated.

Table 5 Type of alleged abuse by gender of child and perpetrator

Type of alleged abuse by gender of child	Male workers	Female workers	Male residents	Female residents
Girls				
Physical abuse only	2	3	1	0
Sexual abuse only	7	2	3	1
Restraint only	3	1	0	0
Physical and sexual abuse	4	0	1	0
Physical abuse and restraint	0	1	0	0
Sexual abuse and restraint	2	0	0	0
Neglect / inappropriate care	1	1	0	0
Boys				
Physical abuse only	14	3	3	0
Sexual abuse only	3	0	1	0
Restraint only	6	2	0	0
Physical abuse and restraint	1	0	0	0
Neglect / inappropriate care	1	0	0	0
Total	**44***	**13***	**9**	**1**

*This number is greater than the total number of adults investigated as different children could report the same worker.

Sex ratios in abuse allegations

Interestingly, the above analysis shows that male workers were marginally more likely to have allegations made against them by boys (57%) than girls (43%), whilst female workers were more frequently accused of abuse by girls than boys (64% compared to 36%). When this is further broken down by type of abuse the above pattern continues for all types of allegations, except for sexual abuse, where substantially more girls alleging abuse by an adult reported a male worker (13 compared to 2). The 2 allegations of sexual abuse made against female workers were both by young women.

In relation to physical abuse male workers were more likely to have allegations made by boys than girls (15 compared to 6), whilst female workers were slightly more likely to be accused of abuse by girls (5 compared to 3). Allegations of inappropriate restraint also showed that male workers were slightly more likely to have allegations made by boys (7 compared to 5), however female workers had an equal number of inappropriate restraint allegations made by both sexes. This pattern of abuse type and sex of perpetrators reflects the sex ratio associated with intra-familial physical and sexual abuse. Creighton (1992) examining the perpetrators of familial abuse, states that the data on sex ratios shows a significant tendency for parents and parent substitutes to injure a child of the same sex as themselves, and sexually abuse a child of the opposite sex.

Allegations of abuse by residents

One-fifth of allegations concerned abuse by other residents. Although this is a significant number, past research undertaken by the NSPCC has indicated that abuse by residents may be more pronounced than is reflected in this study. Westcott and Clément (1992) found that approximately half of the *'lead'* perpetrators of institutional abuse incidents against children were peers. Other studies have identified that abuse by residents is as common, if not greater then abuse by workers (Lunn, 1990; Sinclair and Gibbs, 1998). The problems associated with identifying, reporting and responding to abuse by residents has also received some attention (Barter, 1997). Some US studies, for example the New York State Commission on Quality of Care (1992), have categorised sexual abuse by peers as '*institutional neglect*', thus emphasising the role of workers in protecting children from other residents through adequate supervision. The above study found that in mental health facilities 16% of allegations concerned neglect: child to child sexual contact and that 3% of allegations in their mental retardation (sic) facilities concerned this form of institutional abuse.

Our research found that of the 10 allegations against children 6 related to sexual abuse; the majority of these allegations were made by female residents against male peers. Overall, a quarter of all allegations relating to sexual abuse were against peers. *The Report of the Committee of Enquiry into Children and Young People who Sexually Abuse Other Children* (National Children's Home, 1992), reviewed the studies concerning the incidence of sexual abuse committed by young perpetrators. For the UK studies the percentage of perpetrators under the age of 18 ranged from 28% to 36%.

Only one female child was accused of sexual abuse, indeed this was the only allegation within the research against a female peer. Past research on perpetrators has shown that the overwhelming majority of perpetrators of sexual abuse are male, however women and girls do also sexually abuse children. Kelly, Regan and Burton (1991), for example, found that 15% of abuse by peers and 5% of abuse by adults was committed by girls/women. Creighton and Russell (1995) report a slightly higher rate of 10% for adult females.

Overall, although it is not possible to reach any firm conclusions regarding the above findings, they may indicate that abuse by residents is not generally viewed by local authorities as requiring independent investigation.

Table 6 Nature of abuse allegations

Alleged abuser	Alleged victim	Number of investigations
Single abuser	Single victim	19
Single abuser	Multiple victims	5
Multiple abusers	Single victim	3
Multiple abusers	Multiple victims	6
Multiple resident abusers	Single victim	3
Total		**36**

Relationship of alleged abuser to alleged victim

Over half of the investigations (19) concerned individual children making allegations against an individual worker. Others were significantly more complex. Five investigations concerned allegations against an individual worker by a number of children. Three involved a young person alleging they had been abused by more than one worker, and in 6 investigations 2 or more children alleged abuse by more than one member of staff. In the remaining 3 investigations children reported being abused by other residents, all involving abuse by more than one resident.

Overall 14 of the investigations (not including peer abuse cases) involved 2 or more children and/or 2 or more alleged abusers. In 5 of these cases, at the initial investigation stage only an individual child and abuser were alleged to be involved. Therefore several investigations concerning adults were found to be more far reaching than originally thought.

4 Evaluation of the investigation process

This chapter focuses upon the respondents' perceptions and experiences of the planning and implementation of the investigation, including their evaluations of the initial strategy meetings and determining the appropriate scope of an investigation, through to multi agency working. Within this study it was not possible to evaluate the local authority's initial reaction to the allegation. However, it is important to place the role of independent investigations within the wider context of the local authority's overall response to allegations of abuse. This is covered in the first section of this chapter.

Responding to allegations of institutional abuse

An agency's first and paramount concern should be to ensure the alleged victim is protected from the possibility of any further abuse or retaliation. Additionally the agency must also ensure that other children within the facility, and possibly in other facilities/settings, are also protected.

The initial response by any authority in responding to an allegation should be to believe that the incident could have happened. As Bloom (1992), states it is a commonly held belief that only bad agencies, employing *'sick'* people are involved in institutional abuse allegations. In reality, even if exceptional risk management policies and practices are implemented, this will not free the agency from the possibility of employing a high risk person.

When viewing an agency's response to an allegation, it is important to recognise that its agenda may be separate from that of the investigation teams. The prospect of litigation by the potential victim(s), especially if the abuse may involve large numbers of possible claimants, will be an issue that few local authorities will fail to consider. Dobson (1996), commenting on the Clwyd Inquiry report, blocked from being made public by the council's insurance company, states that the report showed how deeply insurance companies have become involved in the conduct of council investigations into abuse. According to Dobson the report clearly showed how insurers and their solicitors successfully opposed plans by the inquiry team to look for other children who may have been abused. Dobson quotes from a letter sent to the local authority by the insurers:

"Referring to your decision to place notices in newspapers and journals, our experience and that of our solicitors is that such notices only encourage a bandwagon and claims with adverse publicity." (p18)

Dobson also highlights how the insurance companies attempted to restrict the investigation's scope and powers, by reminding the council that it would not be advisable to comment unfavourably on other agencies, as they may also be the insurance company's clients. This should be viewed as a warning to all those involved in investigating this form of abuse, and the implications regarding the independence of such investigations needs to be fully recognised and guarded against. Ultimately, local authorities will generally wish to reduce the likelihood of any possible litigation.

The *Castle Hill Report* (Brannan, Jones and Murch, 1993a) states that litigation by a victim can fall into a number of areas; against the abuser; against the local authority; and against the registration and inspection units. Responding directly and unambiguously in the best interests of the alleged victim is vital, and will additionally lessen the agency's susceptibility to litigation. How an agency responds to an allegation will generally be given more emphasis than the occurrence of the abuse event. In both the *Staffordshire Inquiry* (Levy and Kahan, 1991) and the *Leicestershire Inquiry 1992* (Kirkwood, 1993) detailed attention was focused, and high levels of criticism placed, on the local authority's failure to respond adequately to the consistent flow of allegations made by the children and young people concerned, over prolonged periods of time. Similar issues are emerging in current enquiries concerning abuse in North Wales and the North West of England.

Although it is not possible to evaluate the authorities' initial responses, the research did however find a clear distinction regarding the type of establishments that commissioning local authorities regarded as requiring an increased element of independence. All but 4 of the investigations involved allegations of abuse within local authority residential children's homes.

Of the remaining 4, 2 involved children's homes run by charitable trusts, and 2 concerned suspected abuse in local authority day nurseries. In comparison, Westcott and Clément (1992) studying the NSPCC's involvement in working with young people who had experienced institutional abuse over a 12 month period, found that 52% of the children had been abused within their children home placement, 42% in schools and 5% in other forms of residential settings. Although it is not possible to make any substantive conclusions regarding these findings, they suggest that local authorities are seemingly targeting the NSPCC to investigate allegations of abuse by members of their own social services departments. Abuse allegations in boarding schools, and facilities that provide care for children and young people with disabilities are therefore not being referred to the NSPCC for investigation, although the children are being referred for other services as a consequence of experiencing institutional abuse. Presumably the local authority's own child protection unit will undertake the independent investigation where the school is provided either by the local education authority or is independent. However, the research does indicate that disabled children cared for by social services departments are receiving differential treatment compared to non-disabled children.

The three strands of the investigation process

Investigations into institutional abuse allegations comprise three discrete strands (child protection, criminal and disciplinary). The importance of undertaking all these separately has already been documented within the introductory chapter (although the police investigation may run alongside the child protection one). Within this, the NSPCC investigative role lies solely within the child protection strand. However, investigation team members may be called upon to give evidence in connection with the other two strands, including in a court of law.

Kirkwood (1993) while undertaking the *Leicestershire Inquiry 1992* found that many investigators failed to appreciate the difference between the police objective - the investigation of crime - and their own proper objectives - the investigation and maintenance of correct professional standards. Similarly Rowlands (1993) commenting on an analysis of 50 investigations concerning institutional abuse collected by the Social Services Inspectorate (SSI) found that many did not understand the distinction between the criminal and civil burdens of proof. Within the NSPCC sample, almost all respondents (38) felt that they clearly understood the different levels of proof needed within the three strands of the investigation and the importance of keeping these separate from each other. Most (32) felt that the local authorities concerned also had a clear idea about the differential levels of certainty needed at each level. However, a few respondents (5) reported exceptions. For example one project was asked by the local authority to include on the investigation team a member of their personnel department enabling them to incorporate the disciplinary procedures alongside the child protection investigation. This was refused by the team concerned.

A slightly more commonly reported strategy was for the commissioning agency to ask, if the allegation was substantiated, for the investigators to comment on the eligibility of a worker to continue in their job or to direct the local authority on what action should be taken against the worker. This was viewed by the respondents as placing an even greater level of pressure on them regarding the outcome of the investigations, and is contrary to the guidance contained in *Working Together Under the Children Act 1989* (Department of Health, 1991b).

Strategy meeting

Central to the smooth and efficient running of any investigation is the strategy meeting, as it is in this forum that the investigation's mandate and scope of inquiry are decided, and where lines of accountability and communication are set. In accordance with *Working Together under the Children Act 1989* (Department of Health, 1991b) the major functions of the strategy group are as follows: to consider the need for an emergency protection action if this has not already been taken; to consider whether a joint or individual agency investigation should be pursued; to determine the investigation's scope and allocate resources. However Rowlands (1993) found that many independent investigations in his sample had failed to plan a strategy meeting in accordance with the guidelines contained within *Working Together under the Children Act 1989.*

Nearly every person (38) interviewed in the present study stated that at the beginning of the investigation a strategy meeting had been convened which they, or another representative from the NSPCC had attended. The importance of such a meeting, especially the preliminary one, to ensure the smooth running of the investigation, was emphasised by nearly all these respondents (36:88%).

The importance of such meetings are stressed by Dimmelow (1993):

"Recent SSI inspections of child protection services have revealed very little use of strategy meetings to plan investigations into conventional child protection cases. Such meetings must be seen as essential in responding to allegations of abuse in the residential setting." (p15)

The role of the strategy meeting was generally perceived as being very wide-ranging by the respondents in the study. Overall its role was seen as being to manage the investigation, including deciding initially if the allegation was actually a child protection matter, developing the investigation's remit, including what agencies needed to be involved and at what stages, establishing the principles of the investigation, providing background information and lines of accountability and communication. Central to these discussions should be considerations of whether the referral indicates that the abuse is limited to a relatively few individuals or appears possibly to be more widespread. The meeting must also be sensitive to the possibility that the abuse has an organised element, including the possibility that individuals outside the facility may be involved.

In principle the meeting is supposed to aid multi-agency working, however in practice many respondents (28) had found it to be a highly politicised process. Although respondents frequently emphasised the importance of the first strategy meeting, many felt very unhappy with their own experiences of this meeting. About two-thirds (36) felt that their attendance at the initial strategy meeting should, once they have been thoroughly briefed about the allegation, address the appropriateness of their involvement. Many of these respondents reported that prior to the meeting they often had only limited information concerning the allegation, the amount of work involved, and therefore the level of commitment needed. Unfortunately for a number of respondents their experiences of the meeting did not match their expectations. Some (14) reported that local authorities viewed their attendance at this meeting as signalling their participation, even if this had not been formally agreed beforehand. For example one team which attended the first strategy meeting presumed they would discuss which agency was the most appropriate to conduct the investigation, only to discover that the first item on the agenda was the start date for the NSPCC to begin interviewing the children involved.

Often respondents (22) reported that rather than setting the investigation's agenda at the meeting, they were instead having to fight against having one imposed on them. This was especially difficult due to the difference in status of the other members of the strategy team. As Dimmelow (1993) states:

"Membership of the strategy group is clearly important. At its core there will normally be senior officers of the SSD and Police Authority." (p15)

This is also stated in *Working Together under the Children Act 1989*, which stresses the importance of having senior members of the social services department represented at strategy meetings. Respondents within this study reported that generally the local authority representatives at the strategy meetings were relatively high ranking officials. Although this represents good practice, it also has unforeseen consequences in relation to the NSPCC experiences of these meetings. In contrast to the guidance, NSPCC practitioners reported that they often attended these meetings either alone or accompanied by a colleague of a similar level of seniority. This left many practitioners (15) feeling intimidated by their lack of status within the meeting. Often, senior officers had previously established working relationships with each other, and consequently had a familiarity which added to practitioners' feelings of exclusion and lack of control within the process. Many (11) felt that because of the seniority of the other members their ability to challenge successfully decisions within this context was minimal. Some (6) felt that individual members of the strategy meetings directly nurtured these dynamics to secure a more restrictive remit.

Practitioners who had experienced these problems generally felt that the attendance of someone of at least team leader level or above would alleviate many of these difficulties. In addition it was strongly felt that, if the investigation appeared to be wide ranging, then a senior NSPCC manager should be present. Team leaders also generally agreed that if the abuse was likely to be significant and widespread it was appropriate for a senior manager to be present, at least at pivotal meetings.

Remit and scope of the investigation

The remit and scope of the investigation was a central concern for many respondents (28). Most of these concerns focused on how comprehensive the scope of the investigation should be. This research found that there existed significant differences between respondents regarding how wide they believed the investigation's mandate should be.

The majority of respondents within the study who expressed a view (26) felt that the remit should not simply focus on the specific incident, but needed to be more extensive, thus enabling the wider dynamics of the establishment, including the role of management, to be evaluated within the child protection investigation.

A minority (9) felt that it should be strictly limited to the child abuse event(s) that had been alleged. If other concerns were exposed that were not directly related to the child protection incidents they should be noted but not included in the investigation itself. These respondents felt that an investigation's remit should generally be *'brief focused'*, as they were investigating a specific incident by an individual member of staff. This very narrow approach may not allow the multi-factorial causes that frequently underlie institutional abuse to be uncovered. In the worst case scenario this stance may miss the widespread abuse of children within an institution.

Kelleher (1987) has criticised the *ad hoc* single incident approach to investigating institutional abuse as being highly politicised and based on a crisis mentality. She feels that the focus of such investigations should be on improving the total system, as opposed to examining a particular allegation. The State Institutional Abuse and Neglect Advisory Committee (1987) states that in certain circumstances, due to the nature of some allegations, it may be possible to limit the scope of an investigation. However, generally because of the dynamics of institutional abuse allegations, the investigation should weight on the side of being exhaustive and thorough.

As Doran and Brannan (1996) conclude, the nature of abuse within institutions is complicated and cannot be defined in any simple manner. Similarly Grayson (1988) has also emphasised an ecological approach which can move investigations beyond probing a particular incident to examining the quality of life for all residents. This stance will ultimately enable the development of an abuse prevention programme. If we view this in terms of the definitions provided by Gil (1982), the occurrence of overt or direct incidents of abuse may in fact be a result of the wider care-giving regime, or programme abuse, which may not be identified if a wide ranging remit is not present.

In practice many respondents (24) identified that the remits they had worked with in the past had been too restrictive. Some (4) for example had undertaken investigations without interviewing the alleged abuser. In other instances they had not had the authority to interview routinely other members of staff or children in the facility, or those who had since been moved. Often, although they could interview staff if they wished to be included in the investigation, the remit did not allow them authority to see all workers in private. Obviously for staff to approach a member of the investigation team directly in this way could be very daunting. The problems surrounding *'whistle-blowing'* may still be very pertinent if staff have evidence about an allegation but fear possible reprisals if they are seen to approach an investigation team. By automatically interviewing all staff this alleviates the need for staff to take this initiative individually. This may be particularly important for junior members of staff, see *Leicestershire Inquiry 1992* (Kirkwood 1993), who may be especially susceptible to pressure not to participate.

In contrast Matsushima (1990) states that all persons named as having direct knowledge of the alleged incident need to be interviewed, but that wider *'fishing expeditions'* tend to invite only *'confabulation and curiosity'*. He continues that any investigation arouses anxious reactions within the social system of the residential setting, and children typically respond with upset behaviour. Disturbances to the social system, while unavoidable, should be kept to a minimum.

Although the importance of reducing the level of disturbance within a facility due to an investigation is imperative, Matsushima's assumption that all witnesses can always be easily identified is questionable. Our research found a number of instances when workers who seemed initially to have no direct knowledge about the incident were able to provide important information when they were interviewed.

The present study found that although over half of the investigations (19) concerned individual children and individual workers, others were significantly more complex. Overall 14 of the 33 investigations concerning adult abusers involved more than one child and/or more than one alleged abuser (see Table 6 in Chapter 3 for a further breakdown). In 5 of these cases only one individual child and abuser were thought to be involved at the beginning of the investigation. Hence a significant minority of investigations concerning staff members were found to be more far reaching then originally thought. This should be viewed as justifying the need to have a flexible and wide ranging remit, irrespective of how limited allegations may first appear.

The research also found that investigations sometimes concentrated on the specific event without considering the role of management. As Dimmelow (1993) explains, investigations into institutional abuse have to establish the scope of culpability by determining whether any failures in the general management and running of the home, or the responsible agency, have in any way contributed to the abuse occurring. The scope of any investigation to establish whether this is the case normally goes beyond the brief of a child protection investigation and includes a more detailed and possibly multi-agency inspection of the establishment.

This is reflected by Doran and Brannan (1996) who state:

"The effective prevention and investigation of abuse within institutions is dependent on an ability to understand and address the complex and multi-faceted nature of their internal and external hierarchical and power systems."(p159)

Being unable to secure access to an establishment's management regardless of their seniority, restricts the investigator's ability to undertake a comprehensive and thorough investigation into this form of abuse, and may diminish their ability to place what may seem isolated incidents into a wider management context.

The State Institutional Abuse and Advisory Committee (1987) emphasises that the scope of culpability is far greater in residential placements than in the family context. Culpability, the committee argues, extends beyond the single subject of the report to implicate those directly responsible for administering facilities and programmes. Administrators share the culpability except where it can be clearly shown to have resulted from the personal malice of individual workers.

However, respondents within the present study were also aware that a heavy-handed response, for example bringing in a large scale investigation team for all allegations, may also be extremely damaging to the children concerned. One respondent questioned the use of investigations when the allegation concerned the use of inappropriate restraint. Many (18) felt that the potential disruption caused to the establishment, especially the effect on the children living there, needed to be taken into consideration when deciding how comprehensive a remit should be. However, on balance, most respondents (25) reported that they would have preferred to have a wider remit, including interviewing any staff or child they felt was appropriate.

Suspension

The issue of suspension was highlighted within the research as a significant factor in the investigation process. The grounds for suspending a worker pending the outcome of an investigation are open to interpretation. Official guidance to suspension in *The Children Act 1989 Guidance and Regulations, Volume 4: Residential Care* (Department of Health, 1991a) states:

"Those managing the home will also need to consider what steps are required within their disciplinary procedures with respect to the staff member concerned. It would normally be appropriate for the staff member to be suspended from duty either on the grounds of the possibility of the alleged abuse recurring or concern that his presence might interfere with the investigation. It is also important to ensure that a member of staff in this situation is advised of the need to seek his own advice on protecting his interests in relation to both criminal investigations and proceedings." (para 1.187)

This research found that about half (21) of the alleged abusers who were employees had been suspended during the investigation. The majority of these (15) had been suspended prior to the NSPCC involvement. In 3 cases the decision to suspend was made at the initial strategy meeting. In the remaining 3 cases, the workers involved were suspended after the investigation had commenced. In 2 separate cases this was because fresh allegations were made after the investigation had started, and in another instance the staff member was suspended as his presence was having a disruptive effect on the investigation process. This emphasises the importance of reviewing strategically the decision to suspend staff throughout the investigation process. A disproportionally large number of the investigations resulting in suspension concerned allegations of sexual abuse, indeed this form of allegation frequently resulted in automatic suspension of the alleged abuser (12 out of the 18). Respondents involved in investigating these allegations generally felt that it was appropriate for workers to be suspended during the investigation process. Many (19) spoke about the importance of separating the children from the possible *'grooming'* techniques that sexual abuse perpetrators may have used in the past. This was felt to be impossible if the alleged abuser was still present in this setting. A number of inquiry reports e.g. *Castle Hill Report* (Brannan, Jones and March, 1993a) have documented the very sophisticated and effective grooming technique that workers have used to manipulate children and young people into sexual abuse situations, and to block their ability to seek help. It is important for investigators to remember that this influence will not be easily eliminated, even when the person concerned has been suspended.

Bloom (1992) also argues that suspension should always occur when allegations of sexual abuse are made by children in residential or day care settings, as many children may have their own experiences reawakened. Sexual abuse allegations can have an insidious impact on the residential environment and suspension will often aid in reducing the disruptions and anxiety triggered by such allegations. Other types of allegations, Bloom argues, should have a case by case determination if suspension is needed.

In viewing the use of suspension, it is important to remember that the act itself is not an indictment of guilt. As the *Leicestershire Inquiry 1992* (Kirkwood, 1993) emphasised, it should always be viewed as a routine and neutral act, not as part of a disciplinary process and *'without prejudice'* to the rights of the employee and employer. However, suspension maybe perceived by the suspended worker(s) and the wider staff group very differently in practice. Clough (1996), the General Secretary of the Social Care Association, commenting on the issue of suspension stresses that:

"Fear of what happens when allegations are made against staff is one of the reasons why people do not necessarily blow the gaff. Indeed, I would contend that local authorities are suspension mad. Some actions smack of the most appalling justice on occasions. Constantly, I am told when I appear at an enquiry that the fact that people have been suspended is not a presumption of guilt: the process of suspension is nothing whatsoever to do with reaching an opinion on the case, which I reply 'You tell that to the person who's just been suspended'...I am appalled at what I learn of the way people have been treated from the moment an allegation is made. I am horrified at the number of occasions when people have been totally cleared in an investigation into an allegation but have not been able to go back to the establishment in which they work. The mud sticks." (p144)

Bloom (1992) also fears that the alleged abuser and other staff members will almost certainly view the suspension as a verdict without a trial. This was encountered by the NSPCC investigators who felt that staff often viewed the suspension as a verdict of guilt before the investigation had concluded. Some investigators (15) felt that this made the staff view them with suspicion, and affected their willingness to co-operate with the investigation. Although respondents realised that the act of suspension is in theory an objective one, the fact that the worker will have a record of the suspension left on their personnel file was viewed as contradictory to this theoretical stance, although it was realised why this was necessary.

Bloom speaks about the necessity in such circumstances to constantly reassure staff that the act of suspension is neutral and not an indictment of the worker's guilt. Residential staff also need to be reminded that their primary duty is to protect and advocate for the child. The staff should be informed that, if the allegation is not upheld the agency will do all it can to undo the harm done to the staff member concerned.

In contrast to Clough, who feels that local authorities are too eager to suspend workers with little consideration of the consequences of such an act, various inquiry reports have commented on the resistance agencies have shown to suspending workers while investigations are being undertaken. For example Kirkwood (1993) in the *Leicestershire Inquiry 1992* highlights throughout the report the issue of suspension (see pages 42, 274, 312). Commonly these references are concerned with management's determination not to suspend the alleged abuser if they were possibly able to avoid it. The inquiry found that management failed to appreciate that suspending of the staff member concerned could enable others to speak freely, concluding that the provision of suspension pending investigation needs particular attention.

Warner (1992) states that a possible alternative to suspension is to transfer the worker to another workplace, possibly where no direct child contact is available. Our research found that this strategy was used infrequently. Only 3 workers had been transferred; worryingly in 2 of these cases respondents raised serious doubts about the placement's suitability. Both alternative placements were in other children's homes. In one instance the new setting was in the same street as the alleged victim's own home. Although these are only single case examples, it does highlight the need to be careful when arranging alternative settings.

In the remaining investigations, the workers remained in their place of work while the investigation was undertaken. Two exceptions did exist where workers had already left local authority employment. In the cases where the worker remained within the facility while the investigation proceeded, a number of respondents (24) reported reservations about the situation. Many (18) of these reported feeling uncomfortable with the alleged abuser still working on the premises, feeling it affected the child's perception of how safe they were, and how seriously their allegation was being taken. In one case, although the stress on the worker involved was clearly showing, the local authority refused to suspend him, even though his presence was severely affecting the general running of the home. Eventually the worker went on sick leave. In 3 instances the NSPCC practitioners officially approached the local authority to suggest suspension of the workers involved due to their anxieties. However, these requests were turned down.

Within this research some respondents (9) reported that the young people themselves had asked for the worker to be suspended as their presence was making them feel *'under pressure'*, *'unsafe'*, or *'scared'*. However, in all of these cases workers were unsure what weight the local authority had placed on the young person's wishes. A preferable situation would have been for the young person to have been provided with an independent support person who could advocate on his or her behalf.

Multi-agency investigations

The use of a multi-disciplinary team approach in addressing familial child abuse has been both widely promoted and implemented. In contrast, this research found only limited evidence of multi-disciplinary working in institutional abuse investigations. Moran-Ellis et al (1991) provide a useful classification of multi-agency working that can be used as a reference to classify the NSPCC's experiences. They state that multi-disciplinary working can be viewed along a continuum of collaboration; at one extreme separate working, where no organisational arrangements have been developed, with each agency responding independently; moving along to informal, where although no formalised procedures have been developed, agencies have devised a working coalition; and finally at the other extreme, formal joint working relationships. They argue that in reality different levels of jointness exist at different stages of an investigation.

If we place the 36 investigations undertaken by the NSPCC on to this continuum, we find that only 2 investigations constitute Moran-Ellis et al's definition of formal joint working, where both agencies have acknowledged procedures on joint working, including their respective roles within this. In these 2 investigations the police were present from the initial strategy meeting through to completion of the investigation. Both of these investigations concerned widespread sexual abuse allegations, covering a number of years. The police, social services department and the NSPCC each provided workers to undertake the investigation, with both investigations lasting for a number of months.

However, this does not mean that the police were not informed of other investigations. Over half of the investigations (19) did have a police presence at the beginning, however their participation was minor. Generally, these investigations concerned sexual abuse or more severe cases of physical abuse. The level of informal joint working in all of the above cases quickly fell away when it became apparent that no criminal prosecution was likely to occur, generally due to the lack of substantiated evidence. In some instances (5), the informal joint working at the beginning of the investigation included joint interviewing of the child. This was more usually the case when the allegation concerned sexual abuse. Respondents tended to view this as being particularly important in minimising the potential need to interview the child repeatedly, especially in relation to sexual abuse allegations, thus reducing the risk that the victims may be further traumatised during the investigation process.

In 8 of the investigations, NSPCC practitioners worked alongside colleagues from social services departments, generally child protection officers. However, 2 teams accounted for a disproportionate number of these investigations, having developed protocols of joint working on all investigations concerning out-of-home allegations. Generally, practitioners who had involvement in multi-disciplinary or joint agency working felt that although they had encountered initial problems, including who would co-ordinate and control the investigation process, and what roles each agency should fulfil and lead on, these had lessened over time. Similarly Lloyd and Burman (1996), describing joint police and social work investigations into family abuse, also found difficulties in categorising joint investigation arrangements. Smith's (1989) study based on interviews with 100 practitioners in 6 different areas within the US involved in inter-agency out-of-home investigations concerning sexual abuse allegations, found that without exception the use of multi-disciplinary team approaches vastly improved their response to sexual abuse. However, all of the practitioners interviewed also felt that the maintenance of effective working teams was difficult. They stressed that a multi-disciplinary approach requires constant work and attention and that the operation of the team cannot be taken for granted. The research concludes that difficulties do arise in multi-agency teams, and that it is unrealistic to expect a team to operate smoothly all the time; however, the benefits of such an approach outweighed the difficulties.

Smith suggests a number of basic guides to making team investigations work:

- Firstly, she stresses the importance of open communication in discussing differences of opinion and trying to understand any problems from the other's perspective. Smith emphasises the importance within this of supervisory roles in resolving disagreements.

- Secondly, the need for joint training to enhance role clarification and the responsibilities of each agency is stressed.

- Thirdly, she argues that regular inter-agency meetings need to be conducted to maintain a smoothly operating co-ordinated system.

■ Lastly, Smith states that establishing special units for investigating out-of-home abuse is essential. The benefit of this level of specialism is that staff can receive targeted special training; it also improves efficiency as relatively few individuals in each agency are responsible for undertaking such investigations.

Within this research no respondents mentioned they had been involved in any joint training with external agencies. However many did feel that regular meetings were essential, enabling trust to develop between team members, enhancing the work and relationships within the team generally. In relation to Sharp's last point only 3 projects had established specialised services to investigate institutional abuse allegations. These projects had developed their services slightly differently. In 2 cases projects had initiated this service alongside their other work; in only one instance had a dedicated team been established.

In 14 of the 36 investigations a single NSPCC worker undertook the investigation alone. This may be cause for concern. About half of these workers felt that they would have preferred to have worked alongside another colleague on the investigation. These respondents reported feeling relatively isolated throughout the investigation process, which was frequently seen as being extremely *'complex'*, *'stressful'* or *'challenging'* to undertake alone. Working alongside another colleague, according to these respondents, would have provided the opportunity for mutual and ongoing support. This form of working was also viewed as enabling constant discussion regarding the progress of the investigation to be automatically included in the investigation process. The occurrence of individuals undertaking investigations also has another significant implication. The *Castle Hill Inquiry* (Brannan, Jones and Murch,1993b) states that young people should be able to choose the gender of their interviewers and, if possible, a choice should be given to ethnic minority children to be interviewed by Black or Asian investigators. When there is only one team member, the young people's choice is non-existent.

5 The nature of independence

Independent status

The need for investigations concerning abuse within institutions to be independent from the facilities' management and administration is crucial, ensuring that allegations are objectively examined without any conflict of interest. However this research shows that, even for NSPCC investigators, their degree of independence was seen as a significant area of concern, four-fifths of respondents (34) voiced doubts about how independent they actually were in practice.

It is important to place these anxieties in context before looking at them in detail. All investigators felt they were able to bring greater levels of independence than if the local authority used its own child protection workers to undertake the investigation. Respondents also stressed that the children and young people who had alleged the abuse generally seemed to feel that the involvement of the NSPCC meant that their allegations were being taken seriously by the authority concerned. Additionally many young people (21) had spontaneously told investigators that they were pleased the NSPCC were involved as they would not be biased, because they were not directly connected with the facility.

The degree to which respondents felt their independent status had in some way been compromised varied considerably. Importantly, all these concerns relate to investigating the project's host local authority, particularly if the project had entered into service-level agreements with the commissioning agency. Service-level agreements can be either for whole programmes, where the local authority provides complete funding for a particular service, or agreements that are dedicated to the provision of a service on an individual client basis. The latter was generally found to be the most common approach within this research.

Woodard (1995) states that contracts allow agencies to provide services to clients where the service is either too specialised or too expensive for the contracting administrator to provide. Contracting represents a competitive choice when the contractors cannot open their own programme and there are a number of programmes available. When this happens, the administrator can pick competitively from a choice of suppliers (Teece, 1986).

Independence should firstly mean that projects feel no obligations or pressures to undertake an investigation if they feel, for whatever reason, it may be inappropriate. However, just over half (22) of respondents in the study felt that local authorities placed pressure on them to accept an investigation, sometimes simply expecting them to do so without consulting with the project first. Some local authorities seemed to presume that because the NSPCC is identified in official guidance as being able to undertake these investigations, they therefore have a duty to respond to a request, irrespective of how it may affect the project's other work.

Respondents (23) also felt that refusing a request may have repercussions regarding their wider working relationships with the authority concerned. This fear did not originate from any direct or overt discussions with the agency, but many workers said that the underlying covert agenda, in their perceptions, made this clear. This was seen as being particularly pervasive when the teams concerned had developed some form of service-level agreements with the commissioning local authority. Respondents (19) frequently felt that projects' service-level agreements with commissioning local authorities sat uncomfortably alongside notions of independence. Some (17) questioned how independent they actually were, when to a greater or lesser extent, their project's existence was dependent upon the very local authorities they were investigating.

This is echoed by Francis (1996) who warns that more and more voluntary organisations are expressing their dissatisfaction with the contract culture, stressing that:

"The quest by local authorities to get the best deal from contracts with the voluntary sector seems to be eroding the fundamental principle of partnership. The casualties will not only be voluntary sector creativity and independence, but the clients the services are meant to support." (p27)

Respondents frequently (21) reported feeling worried they may jeopardise their project's relationship with the local authority if they *'rocked the boat too much'*. Generally this referred to either challenging the investigation's scope, or the local authority's lack of response to the report's recommendations (see Chapter 8). However none of the respondents could recall any direct threats being made by commissioning local authorities regarding this. In a number of instances respondents felt that local authorities had approached them with a firmly set agenda which restricted their ability to undertake a comprehensive investigation, but which they had felt pressurised to accept.

George (1994) theorises that the contract culture, and the development of purchaser-provider relationships, is jeopardising the independence of the voluntary sector. He reports that there is some evidence that local authorities are unlikely to fund work which could help clients to take them to judicial review. This is not a shallow concern. As Kramer (1994) states the renewal of contracts is often part of a *'highly politicised process in the community'*. He calls for research to contribute to the policy-making and management of voluntary organisations that seek to maintain their identity and independence while operating largely as providers of public social services in an environment of increasing uncertainty, scarcity and competition.

Some respondents (9) also stated that their projects had developed positive relationships with the local authorities, where each respective body had clear expectations about each other's role, and the level of autonomy NSPCC investigators required. However most reported this had taken a considerable amount of time to develop.

Investigating peers

The issue of investigating peers also frequently arose in relation to independence.

These issues generally centred upon 3 factors:

- Investigating colleagues from the project's local area
- Previous knowledge about a particular facility
- The effect of investigations on the team's wider working practices with local projects.

Although respondents did not generally feel that the hierarchical positions of the alleged abusers significantly affected any of the above issues, it is important to be aware of what levels of seniority were involved in investigations. The position of the alleged abusers has already been discussed in Chapter 3, so a brief summary will now suffice. In 30 cases the alleged abuser was at residential care worker level, 10 allegations referred to residents not workers, 7 concerned were either assistant or officer in charge level and 3 were either domestic staff or in one case an external person. In no cases were management involved at a higher level than officer in charge.

The most commonly stated problem (28 respondents) concerned investigating professionals within the project's own geographical area. This was additionally compounded in many teams by investigating colleagues who were working in a related field to their own. One project for example reported investigating an allegation and then having the alleged abuser attend an NSPCC training course run by one of the investigators. This type of problem was most strongly emphasised by projects who were located in smaller communities, where general contact with the facilities involved was inevitable. This problem is highlighted by Cavara and Ogren (1983) who, although discussing investigations into abuse by foster carers, found that investigators felt uncomfortable at various steps in the process, due to their having to observe closely the work of their colleagues.

Respondents were especially uncomfortable with investigating colleagues whom they knew professionally through their work. In one project this had meant that whilst some members of the team had been investigating an alleged incident, other team members were still working with the alleged abuser in their long-term planned work. In another project the investigation had to be undertaken in complete secrecy from other colleagues within the team as they had previously worked alongside the alleged abuser. Some respondents discussed difficulties in resuming a working relationship with colleagues who had been investigated by their teams, irrespective of the investigations' outcome. This may have implications for the children and young people both parties are seeking to help through their joint working.

A number of investigators (13) also felt that having this previous contact with an establishment, even if this did not include direct contact with the alleged abuser(s), might affect their ability to view the situation objectively. Primarily, respondents expressed concern about bringing preconceptions about a facility into the investigation, and the effect this might have on their ability to be impartial and objective.

In contrast, some American practice literature on investigating institutional abuse (e.g. Grayson, 1988) has argued that the investigators should have a knowledge of the facilities they may be called upon to investigate, including ongoing contact. This enables investigators to have an insight into the general dynamics present in each facility before an allegation is made. Although this restricted contact may be useful, the issues raised in this research indicated previous contact may be inappropriate if this is connected with practitioners' general working role.

In addition 24 respondents were worried that undertaking these investigations within their own areas might affect their wider relationship with colleagues. It was felt that workers who had been investigated might discuss this with colleagues outside their facilities, which could affect the team's relationships with other professionals. About half of respondents (19) felt that if they were perceived as doing these investigations regularly, other professionals would start to view them with caution, fearing they may be accused and investigated next. This might then lead to a *'them and us'* situation affecting the team's wider working relationships.

Eight respondents discussed difficulties in resuming a work relationship with colleagues they had investigated, irrespective of the outcome. This might have important implications for the service users as well as with future joint working. Overall, respondents voicing these concerns inevitably felt this stemmed from investigations in their local areas.

Teams that investigated agencies outside their immediate areas or where they had no contact with facilities due to working with completely different client groups, felt that this made their role as investigators significantly more easy. They felt it enhanced their ability to be impartial and many emphasised that it made the investigation process notably less stressful, not only for themselves but also for the alleged abuser. Interestingly, a minority

(4) who had undertaken investigations into facilities both within and outside their local areas, unanimously felt much more positive about the latter. This has obvious implications for service provision. However it is difficult to determine in any systematic way just how much the investigator's independence was compromised by their wider working relationships with the commissioning agencies concerned.

6 Evidence collecting

Type of evidence

In most of these investigations, there was a lack of physical collaborative evidence. In only a minority of cases (14) did the abuse result in any physical injuries that could be recorded. There was therefore a reliance upon witness statements and the interviews of the alleged abuser and the child involved. It is important to remember that 8 investigations concerned past abuse. Obviously, any physical evidence that may have been present when the abuse occurred would no longer exist. In a further 4 investigations the abuse was both past and present.

Investigators need to remember in cases where criminal prosecutions may proceed, that the investigative process both organisationally and operationally may come under close scrutiny. Interviewing techniques, protection of evidence, and post-interview support are all areas open to examination and workers should be aware of the implications of their actions at all stages. Brannan, Jones and Murch (1993b), describing their experiences of the Castle Hill Inquiry, state that it is crucial that workers are aware of the criminal process and the disclosure of evidence to the defence. They continue that an important element of multi-victim cases is the need to minimise the possibility of the contamination of evidence. Suspected victims should not be given information from previous witnesses, nor engage in group therapy or counselling. From the interviews and the investigation reports in this research, it was not possible to ascertain if all appropriate witnesses to the incident(s) had been interviewed. However, as has already been explored earlier in this report, some respondents felt that the limited remit and scope of their mandates may have resulted in the possible exclusion of potential witnesses who were apprehensive about coming forward. *The Leicestershire Inquiry 1992* (Kirkwood, 1993) states that there was a general failure to identify those people who would be likely to contribute to an investigation's key issues. They continue that in almost every instance, there was a failure to talk to children who may have been able to speak specifically or generally about the complaint.

Interviewing techniques

Due to the lack of *'physical'* evidence within these investigations there was a heavy reliance upon *ex post facto* interviews. In recognition of this, respondents felt that the interviewing techniques used in independent investigations were not only extremely important but also significantly different to family investigations. The major differences revolved around the *'detective style'* interviewing needed in investigating out-of-home abuse, compared to the more *'assisting'* interviews undertaken in cases of suspected intra-familial abuse. In addition, investigations into out-of-home abuse also need to determine the identity of the perpetrator.

Kelleher (1987) describes an agency's response to abuse in family settings as following models of responding both to the immediate abuse incident and to supporting the family unit after the incident has been substantiated. Although these response models may be imperfect, they attempt to deal not only with the abuse incident but with the re-integration of the child into the family unit by helping the family prevent further abuse situations occurring. In contrast, the aim of independent investigations is to decide if it is probable that the abuse did or did not occur. Although prevention may be an aspect, it is not the primary or overriding purpose of the investigation, and this is reflected in the interview process. This difference is supported by Matsushima (1990) and Bloom (1992), who also point out that it is important to remember that interviewing in out-of-home abuse investigations is task-focused; gathering information about an event. The aim is not the development of a treatment relationship or the establishment of an effective identification with either party. Matsushima concludes that the goal of interviewing in cases of institutional abuse allegations is plausibility, with the interviewees consciously trying to reconstruct a verifiable process based on the facts provided for them.

Many respondents (27) in the present research found that the process of reconstructing the event, often in minute detail, made the interview process potentially very difficult, especially as it meant examining extremely closely the young person's description of the events. Many reported that their aim in the interview was to be able to place themselves in the child's position and to view the incident as the child experienced it, enabling the interviewer to see the incident from the child's perspective. This process is also described by Bloom (1992) and Matsushima (1990), the latter for example stating that there needs to be a conscious effort by the interviewer to identify with the perspective of the child by reconstructing the whole episode in its entirety. Many respondents felt that this made the interview process particularly difficult, especially as it meant examining the young person's statement and description of the alleged event in exceptional detail. Frequently, respondents felt that they had already acquired very high levels of expertise in interviewing and talking with children and young people. They placed a very high emphasis upon the need to undertake child-centred interviews. Many spoke about proceeding at the young person's pace, enabling them to discuss the allegations and describe the incident in his or her own words and using non leading open-ended questions.

The Castle Hill Report: Practice Guide (Brannan, Jones and Murch, 1993) states:

"...given the highly sensitive nature of the allegations and the possible abuse suffered, we consider that the pace and direction of the interview should be determined by the young person himself. It was equally important that the young person be encouraged to express in his own words what, if anything, had happened to him. Thus we sought a spontaneous response which was not prompted by leads and hints but what was alleged to have happened to others."

Bloom (1992) emphasises this and states that all allegations, whatever the initial impressions of the circumstances may be, should be taken seriously. The appropriate response is to listen to the child carefully, courteously and non-defensively.

Respondents (25) also generally felt that a similar stance needed to be taken when interviewing the alleged abuser and any other subjects. This again is supported by Matsushima (1990), who emphasises that interviewers should place themselves in the position of both the child and the staff person. In the end, as coherent a reconstruction as possible is sought.

Often in these investigations, no other evidence was present except for the accounts of the incident made by the child and the accused. They were seen as extremely problematic investigations. Faller (1988) found that information about the context of the abuse and the child's description or demonstration of their victimisation could be reliable indicators. This process will firstly use open-ended and then more specific questions regarding possible inconsistencies between accounts. Supporting evidence will provide important insight into the different interpretations of the incident, for example where the event occurred, when and what else was happening at the time. It is up to the investigators to use the interviews, and the possible inconsistencies that arise from the child and staff's perspective, to decide if probability lies with the child or the worker's descriptions of the incident.

7 Issues of support

Nearly all the respondents (34) reported that systems of support were inadequate for the people involved in the investigation, ranging from the alleged victims and alleged abusers, through to the other children within the establishment, the wider staff group, and the complainant's family. Practitioners clearly felt that designating areas of support for all those involved in the investigation process was paramount to the investigation running smoothly and reducing the stress and anxiety experienced by all those involved. It was identified that this should be a formal part of the investigation process, determined at the initial strategy meeting and reassessed throughout the investigation.

Supporting the alleged victim

The majority of respondents (29) felt that it was most appropriate for support to be offered by external professionals uninvolved in the investigation. Many talked about their anxiety surrounding the lack of support for the child involved. Often the NSPCC had been placed in the position of trying to support the child whilst undertaking the investigation. Most viewed this as highly inappropriate, feeling they should be more neutral, but that in the absence of any other forms of assistance or areas of support, felt they had very little choice. In a minority of investigations (6) the child had been supported by their social worker or the local authority's children's rights officer. These cases however seemed to be the exception.

Respondents, in trying to support the complainant, also stated that they were unsure of the degree of confidential information that could be passed to the young person. Many felt that it was important to be realistic and honest with the young person but that this was restricted due to their lack of guidance on what the young person could be told and what was confidential information. Many felt their role should be limited to passing on information to the young person's link worker regarding how the investigation was proceeding.

An organisation of young people who have been in care, Safe and Sound (1996) stress the importance of providing structured support to the young person from the very beginning of an investigation. This will help them to feel confident about making the complaint and reduce the risk of then withdrawing their allegation due to pressure or uncertainty about the investigation procedures.

Respondents felt that the support required by the young people ranged from the need for one-to-one counselling, providing information about the investigation process, updating the young person regarding the investigation, and consulting with the young person to ascertain their views and wishes. However, respondents were generally aware of the very important issues that providing counselling to the young people may entail. Guidance in *Working Together Under the Children Act 1989* (Department of Health, 1991b) for example states:

"Where the police are undertaking a parallel investigation which may lead to prosecution of an alleged abuser, there are important issues to be considered about the need for the child to receive appropriate counselling and support and the need for the child to appear as a credible witness in court." (5.13.2)

The guidance continues that these questions must be examined in the light of each child's individual needs, but ultimately the welfare of the child must be of the first priority. Discussions with the Crown Prosecution Service and psychiatric services will aid in decision making.

Most (34) respondents felt that the best link person to provide this service to the complainant was either the young person's social worker, or the children's rights officer service if the local authority has developed this. *The Leicestershire Inquiry 1992* (Kirkwood 1993) reported favourably on this form of service for young people in care. They highlighted this type of advocacy as being a semi-independent service which is situated outside the formal line-management structure. It could offer a confidential service to young people and, importantly, was directly accountable only to the deputy director, bypassing other levels of the hierarchy.

One other method of support was raised by respondents: the provision of a dedicated helpline. This had been undertaken only in one investigation which involved the widespread abuse of residents over a significant number of years. Many respondents (24) felt that this type of helpline was particularly important if allegations of sexual abuse were to be investigated, especially if this involved contacting past residents, who may not have confronted their experiences since leaving local authority accommodation. The *Leicestershire Inquiry 1992* (Kirkwood, 1993) said the helpline run by the NSPCC throughout their investigation offered valued assistance to victims of abuse who needed confidential counselling, independent of the Social Services Department.

Supporting the alleged abuser

Although most respondents placed priority upon providing support for the young person concerned, many (27) also felt that the alleged abusers were often simply abandoned, with no support being offered from the local authority. Matsushima (1990) and Bloom (1992) similarly stress that, although the agency's first priority must be to protect and support the child, it also has a responsibility to its employee to safeguard their rights and dignity.

Inquiry reports have previously identified the terrible stress that workers are under while they are being investigated. *The Oxendon House Inquiry Report* (Roycroft, 1994) stated, that following the closure of the home in question, almost all of the staff suffered ill health and in a number of cases *'acute stress'* was diagnosed. Similarly the *Ty Mawr Community Home Inquiry Report* (Williams and McCreadie, 1992) states:

"An allegation, whether true or false, against a member of staff of this sort is extremely distressing and disturbing. A member of staff, in our view, has the right to look for appropriate support from his employers. This was lamentably lacking." (p26)

According to Rowlands (1993) the alleged abuser's senior line manager should be assigned to support the staff member, ensuring that their interests are being protected, organising advice and representation via the trade union or staff association and securing professional counselling support if required. The line manager should also update the staff member of the investigation's progress and, if he or she has been suspended, keep him or her abreast of developments in the work place.

Our research shows that only rarely (8) did the local authority appoint a formal link person for the alleged abuser. Even in instances where the local authority did provide such support often this was very limited. Frequently the support seemed to recede as the investigation proceeded.

In a number of instances respondents recalled being contacted by the worker involved to find out what was happening, as they had received no communication from their local authority regarding the investigation. Many of the respondents felt that this significantly added to the pressure of undertaking such investigations.

Other problems concerned the alleged abuser, not being briefed about what the investigation entailed, or how it would proceed. Some had not been informed by the local authority of their right to have support from a trade union. In some instances the local authority had simply told the worker concerned that the investigation was *'nothing to worry about'*, giving a very false impression regarding the seriousness of the situation.

Only 3 investigations involved abuse by residents. This very limited number means that it was not possible in the present study to draw any firm conclusions regarding the support offered or received by this group.

Supporting other children

The research also showed that many respondents felt that the young people within the homes were not being properly supported through the process. Allegations of abuse may be particularly difficult for vulnerable children to deal with, especially if they raise issues relating to the children's own past abuse, and especially if the allegation concerns sexual abuse. Obviously the primary source of support for the young people is through the establishment's staff group.

Supporting the staff group

Respondents often felt that staff reacted with incredulity about the allegation. Many felt that staff perceived the investigation as an over-reaction, particularly if the allegation concerned inappropriate restraint. Some respondents said they had experienced hostility and a lack of co-operation from the staff group while they undertook the investigation. Frequently other staff were unhelpful, manipulative and derisory in their interactions with the investigation teams. Respondents reported various tactics. In some instances staff sought to disrupt the children's behaviour. Some respondents felt that the staff had deliberately *'wound children up'*, directly before they were due to interview them, making them unmanageable in the interview. In another case the staff had *'forgotten'* that the children were due to be interviewed, and had arranged an outing that had to be cancelled, to the children's disappointment.

In another incident residential staff had tried to make the investigation team feel uncomfortable. The NSPCC investigators attended a meal with the children to introduce themselves and answer any questions the children might have before they were asked to participate in the investigation. However staff made the worker feel very uncomfortable and manipulated the conversation to exclude them from any discussions.

Many respondents (23) however felt that homes were often simply *'left to get on with it'*, being offered very little, if any, support from their immediate line managers. Nor was advice or guidance routinely offered regarding their responsibility for supporting the alleged victim and the wider group of children.

The Social Services Inspectorate (1991) states:

"Homes' management should ensure that other staff are supported throughout the disciplinary process and at its conclusion are helped to learn the lessons from the incident and to constructively work through the feelings which may have been created by it." (p29, para 4.38)

Managers of the facilities need to ensure not only that staff are sufficiently supported through the investigation, but additionally need to reduce the risk of retributions from staff and the complainant's peers. Staff may try to dissuade the child from holding to their allegation, or they may distance themselves emotionally from the child (Bloom, 1992). They may experience great difficulties believing the child. Without clear and direct intervention the child may feel isolated, guilty about having made the allegation, and may ultimately feel unable to continue with the investigation, withdrawing the allegation.

The most effective way to reduce the anxiety an investigation may create in an establishment is for the investigation team to communicate to the staff clearly and unambiguously what has been done, and what will be done in response to the allegation. An all-staff meeting should be held as soon as possible following the strategy meeting where they are told what allegation has been made, who has made it and about whom it is made (Bloom 1992). This research suggests that this is an essential element in enabling an investigation to proceed smoothly as it reduces anxiety and enlists the collaboration of the facility's wider staff group.

Some respondents (11) were under the impression that the confidential nature of the investigation meant that neither staff nor the children could be informed about what was occurring, and why they were undertaking an investigation, which was generally viewed as being very damaging to the progress of the investigation. Most respondents (24) however felt that confidentiality did not restrict them from informing the staff team about the details of the investigation.

Safe and Sound (1996) however state that staff should not be told details of the complaint as this will prevent prejudice against the young person while an investigation is taking place. Although this obviously needs to be guarded against, it should not be assumed that the staff group cannot be mobilised to support the child emotionally, in addition, creating an atmosphere of secrecy (except in very particular circumstances) which would not be beneficial to the facility as a whole. The present research indicates that openness is the safest option as this will significantly enhance the collection of evidence. If workers are unaware of what the accusation is they will be unable to determine what is relevant information to tell the investigators.

Lastly, respondents generally felt that priority should be given to emphasising that the staff's main responsibility is to safeguard the welfare of and provide support to the alleged victim. Respondents also stressed that it is important to prepare staff to deal with the anticipated behaviour and feelings of the children. A certain amount of staff members' anxiety may be related to their concern about how the children now will react to them. Staff may also be worried about how to respond appropriately to the children's heightened emotional needs for their support. Many investigators in this study felt that in-service training on responding to abuse allegations would be beneficial for many residential workers.

Supporting and working with the family

The child's family should be informed of the child's allegations and what is being done, including, description of how their child is being protected, helped through the crisis and what services are being provided (Bloom, 1992). The family must be helped to support their child, even if they do not believe the allegation is true. The family may also have to deal with past incidents of abuse which may re-emerge due to the present allegations. This may need specialist expertise. The majority of respondents were unsure if parents had been informed of the allegations. In a number of cases the young person had made the allegation on returning to their parental home for a visit, generally with the family's support. In one isolated case the young person told his parents about the allegation who then informed the agency concerned. However, the young person refused to be involved in the investigation even though his parents were supportive to the claim.

Respondents also discussed their own lack of support whilst undertaking these investigations. Many (27) felt that being involved in these investigations was both *'scary and challenging'* because of the potentially large number of both victims and abusers. Many felt that due to this, senior managers should play a more active role in the process. Managers were viewed as being able to provide support to the team and bring an increased level of authority to the investigation.

8 Post-substantiation issues

The post-substantiation stage of an investigation relates mainly to 2 outcomes; where allegations are found to be true or *'inconclusive but with concern'*. The latter outcome does not imply that investigators believed the accused to be guilty but lacked evidence to prove it. However it does show that although investigators were unable to substantiate the allegation they did have significant child protection concerns relating to general working practices. Allegations that are found to be false or are unsubstantiated also require a formal evaluation of the investigation process at the completion of the work. This study found that in relation to suspected abuse that was either disproved or where allegations remained unsubstantiated, this aspect of the investigation process took place infrequently, and when it did senior managers were often absent from the de-briefing meeting.

A minority (6) of respondents felt that it was not their role as investigators to undertake any further action when they had reached their conclusions about the abuse incident. They felt the objective of the investigation was to determine if the allegation could or could not be substantiated. If the allegation was substantiated it was the responsibility of the local authority concerned to decide what policies and procedures may have contributed or enabled the abuse to occur.

This restricted interpretation of the investigations role was, however, not shared by the majority of those interviewed. Most (31) felt that a central aspect of the investigation was to determine and highlight which policies, procedures and working practices may have contributed to the abuse occurring.

Within substantiated investigations a number of practice and policy factors were commonly highlighted. These ranged from a lack of training and understanding concerning control management, specifically the appropriate use of restraint, levels of staff supervision and support, attitudes to children, communication systems and general levels of staff morale. For example, one inquiry into physical abuse of children by a worker found that the children's home was characterised by a *'macho'* culture that was pervasive throughout the whole establishment. The investigation team found that this milieu had played a major part in enabling the physical abuse to take place. Other authors have also commented on the role of *'masculine'* climates in enabling abuse within institutions to flourish. Colton and Vanstone (1996) from interviewing a number of men who had sexually abused children they worked with, found that abusive behaviour was more likely to be unchallenged, ignored or colluded with, if masculinity was not addressed as an issue within the facility:

"...if the men (and women) in these organizations do not understand the way in which their own definitions of masculinity influence and contribute to the culture of the organization within which they work, they are less likely to be able to identify and respond to situations in which power is abused." (p178)

Perpetrators in the Colton and Vanstone (1996) study describe how their offending behaviour not only survived, but was supported within organisations:

"The primary functions of care and protection were eroded not simply by the behaviour of the skilled lone manipulator, but by the conduciveness of the organizational culture to abuse of power." (p178)

Our research found that sexual abuse was often viewed as being the most intended, involving high levels of manipulation and targeting by workers. In these cases recommendations mostly focused upon how the abuse had occurred, and what policies and practices had enabled or at least failed to stop the abuse from happening. Often reports closely examined the policies and practices relating to staff and child contact, especially in bedrooms and outside the facility where children and staff may not be in the proximity of others.

Investigations relating to physical abuse and/or inappropriate restraint frequently placed a high level of attention upon training, supervision, staff support and involvement in the decision-making processes. Often in these investigations, although the management of a facility was not directly implicated in the abuse, its inability to provide guidance, support and supervision to workers was seen as a significant contributory factor to the abuse occurring.

Investigations concerning allegations of abuse by residents regularly highlighted the level of supervision that residents received, the amount of planned activities, and communication systems between children and workers. Generally, abuse by residents was placed in the wider context of institutional neglect.

Leading on from this, some (26) respondents felt that the report should not simply identify the present policy and practice issues relating to the abuse incidents, but should also contain specific recommendations regarding how standards should be modified or changed to ensure that the abuse would not be repeated for similar reasons. As before, these generally related to issues of improved training and guidance relating to crisis management and particularly restraint procedures, the need for more structured and frequent supervision, training in supervision techniques for managers and greater levels of support for direct care staff. Providing workers with a better understanding of the behavioural and emotional indicators that may suggest that children feel unsafe or unhappy, particularly signs indicating possible sexual abuse, were also identified in a number of reports.

Overall, many (33) respondents stated that the post-substantiation phase of the investigation was *'unsatisfactory'*, *'highly frustrating'* or *'inadequate'*. Most felt that, in comparison to investigations of intra-familial abuse, there existed a lack of post-substantiation procedures. In many cases a formalised process to present the findings of the report, including any recommendations and to evaluate the investigation process itself, was agreed at the initial strategy meeting. However in a number of cases (8), local authority representatives had either failed to attend these meetings, or the local authority representative did not have the necessary seniority to comment on the recommendations contained in the report.

In some instances (11) the local authority concerned had welcomed the report's recommendations. Respondents felt that these local authorities viewed their recommendations as positive contributions to their procedures relating to protecting children from abuse within their residential facilities. However, most of these respondents were unsure to what extent local authorities had considered their practices and policies in response to the recommendations.

Generally, once the local authority concerned had received the investigation report, little or no further contact between the investigation team and the commissioning local authority occurred in relation to the investigation. This meant that most of the respondents interviewed were unable to provide any feedback on how the local authority viewed their recommendations, or if any changes to either policy or practice had followed. However, as most respondents believed that the local authority had not been especially receptive to the reports recommendations, it was felt unlikely that local authorities would have implemented them. One project, for example, had undertaken two separate investigations into the same residential establishment. It was felt that the local authority concerned had not implemented many of the recommendations contained in the initial investigation report, as similar problems relating to practice and procedures were still present in the institution when a second investigation was undertaken.

The fact that this research has highlighted the inadequate procedures for presenting the recommendations and the apparent lack of commitment shown by some of the local authorities concerned, raises serious concerns about how adequately some children are being protected.

Grayson (1988) found that practitioners involved in investigating allegations of abuse in out-of-home care also felt that the intervention phase of the process was both frustrating and limited. She stresses that investigators do not have the same authority over institutions that they do over families. Kelleher (1987) also highlights the problem of intervention. With intra-familial abuse, agencies follow models of responding both to the immediate abuse incident and to supporting the family unit after the incident had been substantiated. She argues that although these response models may be imperfect, they do attempt to deal not only with the abuse itself but with the development of strategies to prevent the abuse occurring again, and the reintegration of the child into the family unit. The same author reports that when abuse occurs in an institution, response models are more limited. In these cases the response is directed towards determining if the abuse incident occurred, with little attention beyond the investigation and substantiation of the incident. Thus, whilst there is a post-substantiation model for family abuse no complementary model exists for institutional abuse. Bloom (1992) stresses that although prevention is not the focus of this form of investigation, it is appropriate to note that the abusive situation should serve as a signal to initiate a risk management analysis of the agency. He argues that this typically is not done.

Respondents in the present research felt that an external element was needed to ensure that local authorities fulfilled their post-substantiation role. One possible solution raised by the investigators was for all reports to be presented to the Area Child Protection Committee (ACPC), who would then be in a position to evaluate the recommendations and monitor their implementation. Another option may be to involve the Social Services Inspectorate (SSI) which could provide an overview in a similar manner.

9 Development issues

Expertise and training

Previous research on investigating institutional maltreatment has unanimously found that a high level of expertise and specialist training is required for effective investigation of this form of abuse. Nunno (1997) emphasises the fact that procedures for addressing abuse within families cannot simply be extended to encompass abuse within institutions. Similarly, Kelleher (1987) highlights the fact that regulations regarding mistreatment were developed for family situations, resulting in significant gaps at the institutional level. The major differences between familial abuse and institutional abuse centre upon the organisational nature of the setting where many unrelated adults and children co-exist. The State Institutional Abuse and Neglect Advisory Committee (1987) concludes that:

"Investigations of allegations of institutional abuse and/or neglect require different investigative skills than one normally possesses and uses when investigating allegations of an intra-familial situation. When investigating allegations of abuse and/or neglect occurring in institutional settings the worker needs to examine the allegation(s) within the context of the policies and procedures of the institution, within the environmental milieu of the institution, as seen from the perspective of both staff and children, and with the added awareness of the physical structures of the institution. All questions asked to staff, the child(ren) named in the report, and other institutional personnel should be set within this new frame of reference." (p68)

Durkin (1982) however emphasises that certain factors and characteristics are common to both intra-familial and institutional abuse. Westcott (1991) surmises that aspects shared by both include isolation, unequal power relationships and denial of abuse. Investigators are therefore not confronting an entirely unknown phenomenon when investigating abuse in out-of-home care settings. Ultimately, workers experienced in undertaking investigations into intra-familial abuse will already possess a basis of expertise and understanding upon which to develop more specific and specialised skills relating to investigating abuse within institutions. However, Durkin also recognises that significant differences are present, for example, that children experiencing institutional abuse will be older, and already part of a select population of children for whom it is difficult to care.

Our research found that respondents had generally not received any specialised training in investigating out-of-home abuse. All had previous experience of investigating intra-familial abuse, with some still involved in this role. However, many (29) were working in projects providing mainly therapeutic and treatment services as opposed to investigations.

The majority of workers felt that the skills they had acquired in relation to family abuse were relevant to investigating institutional abuse allegations. Nevertheless, many respondents stated that they would welcome additional training in relation to investigating institutional abuse. Grayson (1988) also found that many of the workers undertaking investigations were selected on the basis of their general experiences in this field, with few receiving any specialist training.

Respondents felt these investigations were more complex and time consuming than undertaking investigations into abuse within familial settings. This frequently revolved around the possibility that large numbers of unrelated children and adults may be involved in the abusive situation. In addition the bureaucratic situations in which the abuse was embedded was seen as a further complicating factor within the investigations. Many placed attention upon the fact that the abuse may in some way be organised or widespread, and that vital signs which may indicate wide-ranging abuse may be missed. Respondents also stressed that the careers and reputation of the worker involved were *'on the line'*. Many respondents felt that these combined factors, in conjunction with the lack of research and practice literature, made investigating institutional abuse considerably more demanding than intra-familial abuse.

However, respondents (29) also felt that undertaking these investigations was of vital importance, and ultimately very rewarding and, as a respondent said, *'at the sharp end of child protection'*. Respondents frequently mentioned that children within residential homes, due to their challenging behaviour, and the low status of residential care within the UK, were often viewed as a low priority within child protection terms. For many respondents their involvement in these investigations was often viewed as an important contribution to the safety and protection of children within residential establishments generally. In addition, as many respondents were no longer involved in familial investigations they viewed it as an opportunity to ensure that their skill and expertise in undertaking investigations was not lost or allowed to become outdated. In contrast a minority (6) felt that they would prefer not to undertake investigations, either into abuse within families or institutions.

Some respondents (10) also stressed that they had worked in residential settings before moving into field social work. These respondents generally felt that through their past residential experience they had acquired a level of understanding relating to residential care that practitioners who had never worked in the sector may not bring to investigations. This awareness was not simply limited to knowledge of formal policies and practices. These respondents often emphasised the importance of understanding the informal world of institutions. Some questioned whether investigators with no direct experience of residential care would be able to recognise the *'hidden'* practices and dynamics found within this sphere.

However respondents who had no direct residential experience did not generally feel this put them at a disadvantage. Many stated that within their wider working roles they had contact with children in residential establishments and through this had gained some level of understanding of residential care. Some investigators did feel they lacked certain *'common knowledge'* regarding what practices occurred in residential establishments. For example what contact should be allowed between children and adults where no other surveillance is present, such as in the child's bedroom or outside a facility. Respondents also identified that they lacked knowledge surrounding the hierarchical structures within social care systems, especially levels and routes of accountability and responsibility. Others also felt that they lacked insight into the informal world of institutions which may mean they could miss certain signs relating to abuse, for example, how abusive incidents may be *'coded'* in log books or day files.

Training requirements

Lerman (1994) upon reviewing the research states that although there is an emerging consensus that out-of-home investigations of abuse and neglect require specialised expertise and training, the specific attributes of the expertise required is not explored. Although many authors recognise the differences between investigating familial and institutional abuse, few state precisely what training is required to prepare professionals to undertake this role. Our research uncovered a number of training areas that respondents felt would be useful either for themselves or for other professionals working in this field.

Areas of training

Respondents emphasised the importance of workers from different agencies being involved in joint training to provide the opportunity to discuss issues of common concern. As most respondents had been selected for their expertise in familial investigations, it was felt that training should serve to develop and enhance specific skills in investigating out-of-home settings.

Differences between intra-familial and out-of-home investigations

The threshold at which institutional abuse occurs is significantly different to intra-familial abuse, as are its nature and dynamics. Training requirements were seen as centring upon the differences between investigating out-of-home facilities compared to familial settings. These were:

- Parental discretion in child rearing practices are intrinsically broader than in residential settings. A facility's responsibility for meeting designated standards concerning child rearing practices exceed those applied to parents. Consequently, thresholds of significant harm are significantly lower in relation to institutional abuse.

- Factors such as mitigating circumstances, intent and severity, although important in assessing intra-familial abuse, are not relevant criteria for determining whether child abuse or neglect has occurred in residential settings.

- The scope of culpability is greater in residential placements than in the family context. Culpability generally extends beyond the discrete subject of the report to include those directly responsible for administering the facility and its program.

- Maltreatment within institutions includes forms of abuse unique to out-of-home settings.

Residential child care

Policy, procedures and practice

Investigators need to have a clear understanding of what written policies and procedures facilities are obliged to keep and adhere to. Respondents felt that they were generally aware of what policies and practices provided safeguards to children within residential care through their familiarity with both inquiry and review reports. However, they would welcome additional training focusing upon research findings on institutional child abuse and neglect, policy and procedural factors, programme practices and common abuse situations. In addition respondents also felt that training could enhance their understanding of the hierarchical social care structure, especially levels and routes of accountability and responsibility within the social care field.

Informal institutional processes

Some felt that they would like to have a more thorough understanding of the informal processes within institutions, particularly how these informal worlds may impact on abuse. Respondents recognised that it may be difficult to transfer this form of knowledge into formal training processes. However an understanding of general residential working practices and their child protection implications would also contribute to practitioners' knowledge and awareness of the problem.

Restraint techniques

Investigators need to be familiar with the procedures governing the use of restraint on children and young people. The need to have a clear understanding of both Department of Health guidance and the local authorities' own written procedures was frequently stated. Although some guidance on the principles of restraint have been published by the Department of Health, these have in the past been criticised by some as being vague and unhelpful (see Ross, 1994) leaving vulnerable children and staff at risk. Recently the Department of Health has issued further clarification in *The Control of Children in the Public Care: Interpretation of the Children Act 1989* (1997). This new guidance has been broadly welcomed by social workers, although the new control of locking doors has raised some concerns (Downey, 1997). In addition we should not assume that local authorities will have produced comprehensive guidelines on the subject. Bell (1997) states that:

"the absence of national guidelines appears to have made many local and regional authorities reluctant to produce clear and unequivocal advice and guidance to staff about the use of restraint."(p40)

These inconsistencies resulted in investigators sometimes being unclear about what was permissible restraint and what was not. Training incorporating developments in the principles of restraint was therefore viewed as a central area in relation to out-of-home abuse investigations. The importance of understanding the use of restraint within the wider context of conflict management, resolution and control was emphasised as a primary aspect of any training.

Interviewing techniques

Many of the young people involved in these investigations had *'challenging'* behaviour. This has many implications for the investigation process. Investigators therefore need to receive training in interviewing adolescents with behavioural and/or emotional problems.

10 Conclusions and recommendations

The research has looked in-depth at the experiences and perceptions of 41 NSPCC professionals involved in independent investigations. As this is a small sample caution is needed in making any generalisations from its findings. However in the absence of other UK material, its contribution to understanding the process of investigating institutional abuse allegations is an important one. The studies that have provided the context to this research have mostly been from the USA, and the problems associated with transferring messages from these studies has already been documented. Nevertheless, the findings from the present study have generally reflected those found within the US literature, which adds weight to their validity. A summary of the main research findings can be found at the beginning of this report and will not be repeated here.

Child protection challenges

This study has focused primarily upon evaluating the investigation process, the nature of independence, evidence, support and post-substantiation issues. The research findings present a number of challenges to agencies concerned with out-of-home child protection. Overall, the research highlights the lack of both national and local protocols to guide such investigations. In addition the study raises a number of concerns relating to the official guidance governing institutional abuse. The Department of Health's current review of the *Working Together Under the Children Act 1989* (1991b) guidance, including those relating to institutional abuse investigations, is therefore timely.

Strategy meetings

The research identified a range of problems associated with the strategy stage of the investigation. First, there is a need to formulate clear guidance on what procedures need to be undertaken prior to the initial strategy meeting to maximise its effectiveness. Some independent NSPCC investigators felt that they lacked adequate information prior to the initial strategy meeting on which to decide if their presence was appropriate. Despite this, upon attending the meeting their participation in the investigation was viewed by the commissioning authority as automatic. This highlights the importance of ensuring that preliminary discussions are thorough enough for independent agencies to be clear about the level of commitment needed, and that no possible conflict of interest is present. Present protocols already in place to ensure the independence of such investigations need to be built upon. These should include procedures not only to involve an external agency but to ensure they are the most appropriate. Agencies should not be involved in this role if:

- The team has significant service level contracts with the commissioning authority in relation to other services.

- The project have on-going contact with the establishment concerned.

- The team have no knowledge of residential care procedures and practices.

- The team members have no experience of undertaking investigations into allegations of child abuse. The interviewing of children as part of an investigation is based on the principles and guidelines laid down in the *Memorandum of Good Practice* (Home Office, 1992); workers must therefore also have a clear understanding of this if they are to undertake special investigations.

■ The project can only release workers for very limited periods of time due to other planned work commitments.

Another important finding was the issue of status within the meeting. Independent investigators need to guarantee that they are perceived as being of equal authority to the others present at the meetings to ensure that their views and judgements are properly acknowledged. In some cases this may mean that senior managers from the independent agency need to be present at least at the initial meeting to assure that the investigators' independence is not jeopardised. The issue of status may need to be addressed not simply by involving management to a greater degree, but by providing training to investigators to develop heightened skills to cope with hierarchy and seniority. Additionally, these skills would be of value in the wider process of dealing with managers of establishments under investigation, which often involves challenging individuals in authority.

Remit

Respondents were aware of the necessity to balance the need to undertake a comprehensive and thorough investigation against the potential damage that a heavy handed response may have. Consequently the remit of an investigation needs to be tailored to suit its individual requirements. Nevertheless, as this research showed, the investigation's scope was sometimes viewed as being too restrictive. The pressure from commissioning local authorities to restrict the scope of an investigation may stem from many concerns: the wish not to implicate management in the situation, the belief that the children involved are simply trying to make trouble, or that a full scale investigation may be damaging to their service's reputation. This study suggests that safeguards may need to be developed to ensure that an appropriate remit is secured.

A possible protection strategy may entail independent investigators having ultimate authority to decide how wide ranging an investigation's scope should be. This authority should cover a range of issues including suspension, removal of children from the setting and methods of evidence collection. This would mean that not only must their independence be guaranteed, but that the problems surrounding their status within strategy meetings are addressed.

Furthermore, it may be productive to incorporate into the investigation plan a formalised review procedure, thus ensuring that any developments in an investigation are reflected immediately in its scope. For this protocol to be successful a key person within the commissioning authority would need to be identified, generally this should be a senior manager who could ensure a swift response to the investigation's new requirements.

Support

The research has highlighted the lack of support received by those subject to an investigation and documented its effects on the investigation process. This finding suggests that the provision of support should be formally included in the resource allocation aspect of the strategy agenda. Identified individuals or agencies should be assigned to all the participants in the investigation, including the wider staff group and the child's family if appropriate. For both the complainants and the alleged abusers these sources of support should be independent from the residential setting. The research showed that certain residential staff members had been unhelpful to the investigators. This underscores the importance of assuring that not only do staff receive support, but that they are provided with clear guidance on their responsibilities, and appropriate strategies are suggested to enable residential staff to constructively support the alleged victim and the wider resident group. The provision of this service should be formally reviewed throughout the process, and any changes to the investigation's scope should automatically include a reappraisal of support requirements. In addition an evaluation should be undertaken at the conclusion of the investigation to ensure that the support offered was appropriate and to highlight areas that may need to be developed. Once an investigation has concluded, irrespective of the outcome, many of those involved may have longer term support needs that should be addressed by the commissioning agency.

Post-substantiation issues

A major finding from the research, which was reflective of other studies, was the lack of post-substantiation procedures. There existed a general absence of both nationally and locally agreed protocols governing this area. The role of post-substantiation proceedings needs to be formally reviewed by commissioning authorities and independent agencies to ensure that they develop appropriate and comprehensive procedures. Both substantiated and *'inconclusive but with concern'* outcomes should result in a post-substantiation phase. The latter outcome does not imply that investigators believed the accused to be guilty but lacked evidence to prove it. However it does show that although investigators were unable to substantiate the allegation they did have significant child protection concerns relating to the workers' general working practices. The research suggests that both substantiated and *'inconclusive but with concern'* outcomes should be accompanied with a detailed breakdown of the following issues:

- Assessment of culpability of wider staff group and management.

- Identification of any policies, procedures, safeguards and working practices that either directly or indirectly facilitated or enabled the abuse to occur.

- Recommendations regarding how policies, procedures and practices should be modified or changed to ensure that abuse does not occur in the future.

The above evaluations and recommendations would be presented to the commissioning agency for discussion at the post-substantiation meeting. The timetable to undertake this should be decided at the initial strategy meeting, as should confirmation of which members of the meeting will attend. This ought to include senior members of the social services department and senior managers responsible for the residential setting involved. The post-substantiation phase should also evaluate the investigation process itself, and identify any practices or procedures that may need to be improved or enhanced.

However, concerns were also raised about commissioning authorities' level of response to recommendations for practice following a substantiated or *'inconclusive but with concern'* finding. An external element may be necessary to guarantee that local authorities fulfilled their post-substantiation role. One possible solution may be for all reports to be presented to the Area Child Protection Committee (ACPC), which would then be in a position to evaluate the recommendations and monitor their implementation. Another option may be to involve the Social Services Inspectorate (SSI) which could provide an overview in a similar manner.

Unsubstantiated allegations

Post investigation procedures are equally important when an allegation has been found to be untrue. This was not raised as an issue in the present research, perhaps because the investigators felt that there was no further role for them in these circumstances, or because this was seen as less important than the lack of procedures when the investigation had identified causes for concern. Nevertheless an investigation will leave a residue of problems and feelings which need to be addressed, even if no abuse is thought to have occurred. Those involved will need to be informed of the outcome of the investigation, there may need to be consideration of whether they should still work or live together, and of the action to be taken to resolve any difficulties between them. Failure to deal with such issues has been found in some enquiries to be a problem which led to considerable complications and unhappiness for all involved (Williams and McCreadie, 1992). The strategy should include provision for responsibility for any follow up activity needed by the authority with responsibility for the child, the establishment or both, in the event of an allegation being unfounded.

Models for an independent investigation service

A major finding of the study concerned NSPCC investigators' perceptions of independence. Many felt that projects' service-level agreements sat uncomfortably alongside notions of independence. In addition, investigating colleagues in the teams' local area was identified as being particularly difficult. Respondents who had undertaken investigations outside their local areas, or where a dedicated service had been established, described fewer problems relating to independence. This has important consequences for service provision for all agencies providing independent investigation services. A number of options for service developments are suggested.

These were developed within the NSPCC structure of a national organisation with regional centres. They would need modification for use by agencies with different structures.

- Neighbouring projects could pool resources, identifying within each team a number of workers who have a range of specialised skills to undertake independent investigations. This model of provision would relieve the problem of teams investigating their own local authority. However, due to the time and personnel commitment independent investigations require, teams would need to prioritise this as a key area of work and acknowledge that these investigations may disrupt their longer planned work.

- Regional centres could develop a specialised and dedicated service to undertake investigations in their regions. Although the benefits in relation to independence are obvious, the level of demand within a region would be a determining factor in its feasibility.

- A national service could be developed to undertake independent investigations throughout England and Wales. This would alleviate the above problems and the team could be chosen to ensure a wide range of expertise and knowledge. However demand could mean that outside personnel might need to be brought in at certain points. This could affect the team's ability to respond quickly to a request. The research also found that an important aspect of an investigation was the development of trust between team members. When this involved multi-disciplinary investigations this sometimes took a significant period of time. A national service would therefore need constantly to re-establish working relationships with external professionals throughout England and Wales, which could be both demanding and time consuming.

Review of present guidance

Since this present research started, two major reviews of the safeguards for children living away from home have been published (Department of Health and Welsh Office, 1997; Scottish Office, 1997) and a consultation document has been issued to consider changes in guidance on interagency co-operation to protect children (Department of Health, 1998). The findings from this research have implications for the intended revision of the guidance.

Independence

Working Together Under the Children Act 1989 (Department of Health, 1991b) states:

"Investigations of allegations or of suspicions of abuse by a member of the SSD's own staff should, as far as possible, include an independent element. This could, for example, be a representative from another SSD or the local NSPCC." (5.20.6)

The reviews of safeguards and consultation document on *'Working Together'* endorse the need for independence, and suggest ways of achieving it. The consultation document, for example, suggests that child protection investigations in residential settings may be complex, and require particular expertise and experience. It invites views on whether there should be local dedicated groups of suitably trained and experienced police officers and social workers (Department of Health, 1998, para 5.18).

The results of the present research suggest that there will often be circumstances in which independence can best be assured by commissioning investigations from outside the local area. Staff from local statutory and voluntary agencies are involved in the course of their work in interagency collaboration at many levels, not solely that of child protection. They may have previously worked as colleagues and co-workers, and voluntary agencies may be involved in provision of contractual services to a local authority. Staff may have had contact through local professional networks, professional associations, or joint training. These situations can place a strain on staff who are asked to investigate allegations against present or future colleagues in other agencies, and could compromise, or appear to compromise, the independence of the investigation. Guidance should address this possibility and require it to be considered in commissioning investigations.

The involvement of local police in specialist teams may have particular difficulties in the case of young people who have records of previous offending, both when the young people are making allegations of abuse and when they are themselves suspected of abusing other children. Previous contact may damage the relationship of trust which is needed between young people who have been victims of abuse and investigators, and pre-formed attitudes may affect the judgement of investigators. This has proved to be a problem in some of the most serious incidents of abuse of young people in residential care, leading to a reluctance to believe allegations when the victim was regarded as troublesome or unreliable.

■ Recommendation

Guidance should include more detailed advice on securing independence within independent investigations by choice of agencies. When planning an investigation consideration should be given as to whether an independent investigation should be carried out by staff from a different area who have no previous or likely future contact with either the children or the professionals involved. Voluntary and other independent agencies providing investigation services should be prepared to deploy teams from outside the area of the current investigation when appropriate.

Children's wishes

In addition *The Children Act 1989 Guidance and Regulations, Volume 4: Residential Care* (Department of Health, 1991a) states:

"It is essential that a relationship is built up between children and staff such that children feel that they can trust staff to do the best thing with a disclosure of abuse. This means that a child feels his or her wishes about what should happen are taken into account and that the consequences of disclosure do not make matters worse for the child." (1.182)

■ Recommendation

A child's wish to have their allegation investigated by an independent agency should be considered. Children and young people should be made aware of this, including the reasons why an enhanced independent element may be an advantage in certain circumstances, so they can make an informed decision and their wishes can be fully acknowledged. In addition, if the local authority decide that an independent agency is not required the child should be informed on what basis this decision was reached. This should also be noted in the final investigation report.

Remit

Working Together under the Children Act 1989 (Department of Health, 1991b) states:

"It must also be recognised that there may be abuse by staff in a residential setting which pervades the whole staffing fabric with the involvement and collusion of several, possibly senior, members of staff." (5.20.7)

The above paragraph recognises the importance of an investigation's scope and the need to consider the possibility that senior members of staff may be implicated in the abuse. The present research illustrates the difficulties which can arise when investigations come to suspect that abuse may be widespread in a particular residential setting or service, but have a remit only to investigate the original allegation. The possibility of collusive practice covering up such abuse to protect staff or agencies is acknowledged, both in *People Like Us* (Utting, 1997) and in the consultation document on *Working Together Under the Children Act 1989* (Department of Health, 1991b). However guidance should include specific guidelines on ensuring that an appropriate remit is secured.

■ Recommendation

Guidelines should recognise that processes may be present to restrict an investigation's scope, and provide specific safeguards to ensure this risk is minimised. These safeguards should recognise that independent investigators ought to have ultimate authority over the scope of a special investigation, and that the remit should be determined in a flexible and responsive manner.

Strategy discussion and planning

Working Together Under the Children Act 1989 (Department of Health, 1991b) states that an early strategy discussion between the statutory agencies should be held to plan the investigation, and that this will not necessarily require a meeting (5.13.1). This implies that the discussion should involve those with a formal part to play in the investigation. The consultation document on *Working Together* recognises that communication between agencies will not be adequately covered in one discussion and invites views on the form that discussions should take.

In independent investigations the single strategy meeting proved to have some difficulties when there was uncertainty about the role of the independent agency at the outset, or when potential investigators were invited to a strategy meeting in advance of the decision to commission the independent investigation. Independent investigators thought it necessary for social services departments to brief potential investigators and discuss remit before the agency could decide whether it should take on the investigation, or the detailed investigation was planned. There were sometimes uncertainties over the nature and form of feedback from independent investigators to the statutory agencies.

■ Recommendation

Where an independent investigation is being considered, planning will require three stages: firstly, a preliminary strategy discussion to clarify whether an independent investigator should be appointed and which agencies might be appropriate to invite to carry it out; secondly, the appointment, clarification of the remit and full briefing of the independent agency; and lastly, a meeting with all agencies involved to plan the investigation.

Support

The Children Act 1989 Guidance and Regulations, Volume 4: Residential Care (Department of Health, 1991a) states that:

"Staff need supervisory or managerial support to deal effectively with this process and avoid defensiveness ...It is important that staff in the children's home co-operate fully with external investigators in order that the full extent of abuse is discovered and that the children caught up in the problem receive proper counselling." (1.185)

The above guidance continues that:

"It is also important to ensure that a member of staff in this situation is advised of the need to seek his own advice on protecting his interests in relation to both criminal and disciplinary investigations and proceedings." (1.187)

■ Recommendation

The above highlights the prominence placed on support within the official guidance. Nevertheless this research indicates that the provision of support needs to be strengthened within special investigations through formally incorporating it in the strategy agenda.

Post-substantiation issues

Official guidance governing special investigations does not include any reference to the post-substantiation stage.

■ Recommendation

It is important that guidance should include post-substantiation protocols describing their role and emphasising their importance for prevention.

Conclusion

The role of independent investigators constitutes an important commitment to safeguarding children living away from home. It may not be possible to stop all abuse incidents before they occur however, if children feel able to report their victimisation, due to appropriate, sensitive and supportive investigation procedures, this will make a significant contribution to ensuring that the tragedies of the past are not repeated. Research needs to contribute to this process by providing a basis upon which child protection professionals can build upon their existing knowledge to develop a body of expertise relating to investigating allegations of institutional abuse. It is only through a widespread and consistent commitment to safeguarding the welfare of children in residential facilities that they will be protected from maltreatment, enabling confidence and morale to be restored to this pivotal component of out-of-home care.

References

★ Denotes UK literature

Balloch, S., Andrew, T., Ginn, J., McLean, J., Pahl, J. and Williams, J. (1995). **Working in the Social Services.** London: National Institute for Social Work, Research Unit.★

Barter, C. (1997). Who's to blame: conceptualising institutional abuse by children. *Early Child Development and Care, 133,* 101-114.★

Bell, L. (1997). The physical restraint of young people. *Child and Family Social Work, (1),* 37-47.★

Berridge, D. and Brodie, I. (1996). Residential child care in England and Wales: the inquiries and after. In M. Hill and J. Aldgate (Eds) **Child Welfare Services: Developments in Law, Policy, Practice and Research.** London: Jessica Kingsley.★

Berridge, D. and Brodie, I. (1998). **Children's Homes Revisited.** London: Jessica Kingsley.★

Besharov, D. J. (1988). **Child Abuse and Neglect Report and Investigation.** Washington, DC: American Bar Association.

Blatt, E. (1990). Staff supervision and the prevention of institutional abuse and neglect in residential care settings. *Journal of Child and Youth Care, (4),* 73-80.

Blatt, E. (1992). Factors associated with child abuse and neglect in residential care settings. *Children and Youth Services Review, (14),* 493-517.

Blatt, E. and Brown, S. (1986). Environmental influences on incidents of alleged child abuse and neglect in New York State psychiatric facilities: toward an ecology of institutional child maltreatment. *Child Abuse and Neglect, (10),* 171-180.

Bloom, R.B. (1992). When staff members sexually abuse children in residential care. *Child Welfare, (2),* 131-145. Article based on paper presented at the annual meeting of the American Association of Children's Residential Centers in St. Petersburg, FL, November 1990.

Brannan, C., Jones, J.R. and Murch, J.D. (1993a). **Castle Hill Report: Practice Guide.** Shrewsbury: Shropshire County Council.★

Brannan, C., Jones, J.R. and Murch, J.D. (1993b). Lessons from a residential special school enquiry: reflections on the Castle Hill Report. *Child Abuse Review, 2,* 271-275.★

Cavara, M. and Ogren, C. (1983). Protocol to investigate child abuse in foster care. *Child Abuse and Neglect, 7(3),* 287-295.

Children Act 1989. Chapter 41. London: HMSO.

Clough, D. (1996). Uncovering abuse. In R. Clough (Ed) **The Abuse of Care in Residential Institutions.** London: Whiting and Birch.★

Colton, M. and Vanstone, M. (1996). **Betrayal of Trust: Sexual Abuse by Men Who Work With Children...In Their Own Words.** London: Free Association Books.★

Creighton, S. (1992). **Child Abuse Trends in England and Wales 1988-1990: And an Overview from 1973-1990.** London: NSPCC.*

Creighton, S. and Russell, N. (1995). **Voices From Childhood: A Survey of Childhood Experiences and Attitudes to Child Rearing Among Adults in the United Kingdom.** London: NSPCC.*

Davidson, H. A. (1988). Abuse in out-of-home care: recent statutory and agency responses. In D. J. Besharov (Ed) **Protecting Children from Abuse and Neglect: Policy and Practice.** Springfield, Illinois: Charles C. Thomas.

Department of Health, (1991a). **The Children Act 1989 Guidance and Regulations, Volume 4: Residential Care.** London: HMSO.*

Department of Health, Home Office, Department of Education and Science, Welsh Office, (1991b). **Working Together Under the Children Act 1989: A Guide to Arrangements for Inter-agency Co-operation for the Protection of Children from Abuse.** London: HMSO.*

Department of Health, (1991c). **The Children Act 1989 Guidance and Regulations, Volume 5: Independent Schools.** London: HMSO.*

Department of Health, (1991d). **The Children Act 1989 Guidance and Regulations, Volume 6: Children with Disabilities.** London: HMSO.*

Department of Health, (1991e). **Children in the Public Care: A Review of Residential Child Care by Sir William Utting.** London: HMSO.*

Department of Health, (1992). **Choosing with Care: Report of the Committee of Enquiry into the Selection, Development and Management of Staff in Children's Homes, Chaired by Sir Norman Warner.** London: HMSO.*

Department of Health, (1995a). **Child Protection: Messages from Research.** London: HMSO.*

Department of Health, (1995b). **Children Looked After by Local Authorities. Year Ending 31 March 1995.** London: HMSO. *

Department of Health, (1997). **The Control of Children in the Public Care: Interpretation Of The Children Act 1989.** London: Social Services Inspectorate Department of Health.*

Dimmelow, C. (1993). Child protection: particular requirements in residential care. In **The Effects on Residential Child Care Staff of Investigations of Abuse.** Paper presented at Crossmeads Conference Centre, Exeter, 18 October 1993. Social Services Inspectorate.*

Dobson, R. (1996). Gagged! *Community Care,* 2-8 May 1996, 18-19.*

Doran, C. and Brannan, C. (1996). Institutional abuse. In P. C. Bibby (Ed) **Organised Abuse: The Current Debate.** London: Arena.*

Dodge-Reyome, N. (1990). Executive directors' perceptions of the prevention of child abuse and maltreatment in residential facilities. *Journal of Child and Youth Care, 4,* 45-60.

Downey, R. (1997). Staff give guarded welcome to new restraint guidelines. *Community Care,* 27 February-5 March, 1997, 3.*

Durkin, R. (1982). Institutional child abuse from a family systems perspective: a working paper. In R. Hanson (Ed) **Institutional Abuse of Children and Youth.** New York: The Haworth Press.

Durkin, R. (1982). No one will thank you: first thoughts on reporting institutional abuse. *Child and Youth Services, 4(12),* 109-113.

Faller, K. (1988). Criteria for judging the credibility of children's statements about their sexual abuse. *Child Welfare, 67 (5)* (Sept-Oct 1988), 389-401.

Francis, J. (1996). Creative casualties. *Community Care,* 12-18 September 1996, 26-27.*

George, M. (1994). Contract killers. *Community Care,* 2-8 June, 26-27.*

Gil, E. (1982). Institutional abuse of children in out-of-home care. In R. Hanson (Ed) **Institutional Abuse of Children and Youth.** New York: The Haworth Press.

Grayson, J. (1988). Abuse and neglect in out-of-home care. *Virginia Child Protection Newsletter, 25,* Spring 1988. Virginia: Department of Social Services, Bureau of Child Protection Services.

Groze, V. (1990). An exploratory investigation into institutional mistreatment. *Children and Youth Services Review, 12,* 229-241.

Home Office in conjunction with Department of Health, (1992). **Memorandum of Good Practice on Video Recorded Interviews with Child Witnesses for Criminal Proceedings.** London: HMSO.*

Kelleher, M. E. (1987). Investigating institutional abuse: a post-substantiation model. *Child Welfare, 66,* 343-351.

Kelly, L. (1992). The connections between disability and child abuse: a review of the research evidence. *Child Abuse Review, 1,* 157-167.*

Kelly, L., Regan, L. and Burton, S. (1991). **An Exploratory Study of the Prevalence of Sexual Abuse in a Sample of 16-21 Year Olds.** PNL: Child Abuse Studies Unit.*

Kirkwood, A. (1993). **The Leicestershire Inquiry 1992.** Leicester: Leicestershire County Council.*

Kramer, R. (1994). Voluntary agencies and the contract culture: "dream or nightmare?" *Social Services Review, 68(1),* March 1994.*

Lerman, P. (1994). Child protection and out-of-home care: system reforms and regulating placements. In G. B. Melton and F. D. Barry (Eds). **Protecting Children from Abuse and Neglect: Foundations for National Strategy.** New York: Guildford Press.

Levy, A. and Kahan, B. (1991). **The Pindown Experience and the Protection of Children.** Stafford: Staffordshire County Council.*

Link, (1996). Issue 6. London: NSPCC.*

Lloyd, S. and Burman, M. (1996). Specialist police units and the joint investigation of child abuse. *Child Abuse Review, 5(1),* 4-17. *

Lunn, T. (1990). Pioneers of abuse control. *Social Work Today, (3)22,*13 September, 9.*

Marchant, R. and Page, M. (1992). Bridging the gap: investigating the abuse of children with multiple disabilities. *Child Abuse Review, 1,* 179-183.*

Matsushima, J. (1990). Interviewing for alleged abuse in the residential treatment centre. *Child Welfare, 69,* 321-331.

Mercer, M. (1982). Closing the barn door: the prevention of institutional abuse through standards. *Child and Youth Services, 4,* 127-132.

Moran-Ellis, J., Conroy, S., Fielding, N. and Tunstill, J. (1991). **Investigation of Child Sexual Abuse. An Executive Summary.** Guildford: University of Surrey.*

National Association of Young People in Care, (1989). **Report on Violations of the Basic Human Rights of Young People in Care of London Borough of Greenwich and other Local Authorities.** London: NAYPIC.*

National Children's Home, (1992). **The Report of the Committee of Enquiry into Children and Young People who Sexually Abuse other Children.** London: NCH.*

New York State Commission on Quality of Care, (1992). **Child Abuse and Neglect in New York State Office of Mental Health and Office of Mental Retardation and Developmental Disabilities Residential Programs.** New York State: Commission on Quality of Care for the Mentally Disabled.

Nunno, M. (1997). Institutional abuse: the role of leadership, authority and the environment in the social services literature. *Early Child Development and Care, 133,* 21-40.

Nunno, M. and Rindfleisch, N. (1991). The abuse of children in out-of-home care. *Children and Society, 5(4),* 295-305.

Osborne, J. (1996). Managing enquiries. In R. Clough (Ed) **The Abuse of Care in Residential Institutions.** London: Whiting and Birch.*

Pringle, K. (1992). Child sexual abuse perpetrated by welfare personnel and the problem of men. *Critical Social Policy, 12(3),* issue 36, 4-19.*

Rindfleisch, N. (1990). Reporting out-of-home abuse and neglect incidents: a political-contextual view of the process. *Journal of Child and Youth Care, (4) 6,* 61-72.

Rindfleisch, N. and Baros-Van Hull, J. (1982). Direct careworkers' attitudes toward the use of physical force with children. *Child and Youth Services, 4,* 115-125.

Rindfleisch, N. and Rabb, J. (1984a). Dilemmas in planning for the protection of children and youths in residential facilities. *Child Welfare, 63,* 205-215.

Rindfleisch, N. and Rabb, J. (1984b). How much of a problem is resident mistreatment in child welfare institutions? *Child Abuse and Neglect, 8,* 33-40.

Rosenthal, J., Motz, J., Edmonson, D. and Groze, V. (1991). A descriptive study of abuse and neglect in out of home placement. *Child Abuse and Neglect, 15,* 249-260.

Ross, S. (1994). Coping with children's challenging behaviour in care. *Scolag, 215,* 114.*

Rowlands, J. (1993). Policies, procedures and guidance: the established wisdom. In **The Effects on Residential Child Care Staff of Investigations of Abuse.** Paper presented at Crossmeads Conference Centre, Exeter, 18 October 1993. Social Services Inspectorate.*

Roycroft, B. (1994). **Oxendon House: A Case to Answer? Report of the Independent Inquiry.** August 1994. Bedfordshire County Council.*

Safe and Sound, (1995). **So Who are We Meant to Trust Now?** London: NSPCC.*

Scottish Office, (1997). **Children's Safeguard Review** by Roger Kent. Scottish Office: Edinburgh.*

Sinclair, I. and Gibbs, I. (1998). **Children's Homes: A Study in Diversity.** Chichester: John Wiley.*

Sloan, J. (1988). Professional abuse. *Child Abuse Review, 2(3),* 7-8.

Smith, B. E. (1989). The multidisciplinary team approach to investigating out-of-home child sexual abuse cases. *Response, 12,* 10-12.

Social Services Inspectorate, (1991). **Safe from Abuse? An Inspection of Community Homes in Leicestershire.** London: Department of Health.*

Spencer, J. W. and Knudsen, D. (1992). Out of home maltreatment: an analysis of risk in various settings for children. *Children and Youth Services Review, (14),* 485-492.

State Institutional Abuse and Neglect Advisory Committee, (1987). **Specialized Training in the Investigation of Out-of-Home Child Abuse and Neglect.** Paper prepared for The Interagency Project on Preventing Abuses in Out-of-Home Child Care Settings. Colorado: Division of Family and Children's Services, Department of Social Services.

Sundrum, C. (1984). Obstacles to reducing patient abuse in public institutions. *Hospital and Community Psychiatry, 35,* 238-243.

Support Force for Children's Residential Care, (1995). **Final Report to the Department of Health.** London: Department of Health.*

Teece, D. J. (1986). Profiting from technological innovation: implications for integration, collaboration, licensing and public policy. *Research Policy, 15,* 285-305.

Thomas, G. (1982). The responsibility of residential placements for children's rights to development. In R. Hanson (Ed) *Institutional Abuse of Children.* New York: The Haworth Press.

Thomas, G. (1990). Institutional child abuse: the making and prevention of an un-problem. *Journal of Child and Youth Care, 4(6),* 1-22.

Utting, Sir W. (1997). With Department of Health and Welsh Office. **People Like Us: The Report of the Review of the Safeguards for Children Living Away From Home.** London: HMSO.*

Westcott, H. (1991). **Institutional Abuse of Children - From Research to Policy: A Review.** London: NSPCC.*

Westcott, H. and Clemént, M. (1992). **NSPCC Experience of Child Abuse in Residential Care and Educational Placements: Results of a Survey**. London: NSPCC.*

Westcott, H. and Cross, M. (1996). **This Far and No Further: Towards Ending the Abuse of Disabled Children.** London: Venture Press.*

Williams, G. and McCreadie, J. (1992). **Ty Mawr Community Home Inquiry.** Cwmbran: Gwent County Council.*

Woodard, K. L. (1995). Introduction and acceptance of inter-organisational agreements: the experience of seventy-five administrators in one county. *Administration in Social Work, 19(4),* 51-81.